Primary Education
Issues for the Eighties

Primary Education
Issues for the Eighties

Edited by
COLIN RICHARDS

ADAM & CHARLES BLACK LTD · LONDON

First published 1980
A & C Black (Publishers) Ltd
35 Bedford Row, London WC1R 4JH
© 1980 A & C Black (Publishers) Ltd

ISBN 0 7136 2068 4

Primary education.
  1. Education, Elementary — Great Britain
  I. Richards, Colin
  372.9'41   LA633

  ISBN 0 7136 2068 4

Text set in 11/13 pt VIP Bembo, printed and bound
in Great Britain at The Pitman Press, Bath

Contents

CONTENTS

Introduction

This book seeks to highlight issues, opportunities and possibilities for the development of primary education in the 1980s.
It does this by developing further some of the issues raised in
the HMI national primary survey and by examining others of
significance with which the survey does not deal. The book
does not take a 'party line' on primary education; it does not
represent the views of any one interest group; it does not
advocate any one set of policies or practices. Its contributors
are a diverse group drawn, with one important exception, from
different educational agencies concerned with the primary
years; they are united, however, in the importance they attach
to primary education as primary *education* and in their willingness to contribute to its constructive reappraisal—a reappraisal
rendered especially necessary by the critical situation facing
primary schools. It was the changing situation facing primary
education which gave rise to this book.

The changes provide the general context for the individual
chapters which follow. It is not easy to characterise them
succinctly; changes in education (as in society generally) rarely
occur in clear-cut, tidy, unequivocal ways. The notion of
'dominant themes' may prove useful in providing an overall
perspective. It can be argued that in the period 1967–79 policy
and, to a lesser but unknown extent, practice in primary
education have been influenced by a number of themes and
that these themes have changed over the years so that the
dominant themes of the later '60s are not those of the late '70s
(and probably the early '80s).

A decade ago *expansion* was a dominant theme. There was

demographic expansion with a particularly large increase in the number of primary school pupils between 1965 and 1970. There was economic expansion which led to an increase in the resources allocated to education and in turn to primary education. There was expansion in political and public expectations regarding the part education could play in fostering policies such as the promotion of greater equality of opportunity, the enhancement of economic growth and the regeneration of inner-cities. Today *contraction* is a dominant theme. There has been a sharp demographic decline (Chapter 13), much of which has yet to affect the schools. There has been economic decline with corresponding reductions in educational expenditure which *have* affected schools. In particular there has been public and political disillusionment with education; the latter has not produced the social and economic benefits which were hoped for and which those of us in education did not dispute at the time. Overall, the last four years have seen a marked contraction in expectations.

Contraction in pupil numbers forms the backcloth to all the chapters in this book and is the specific focus of Howard Collings' contribution which provides facts, projections and possible implications and of Roy Storrs' assessment of the opportunities, problems and strategies open to us in a contracting roll situation. A number of authors stress the positive as well as the problematic aspects of contraction—increased space, greater opportunity for individual assessment and help (Tom Marjoram) and the possibility of providing more appropriate, demanding curricula (Norman Thomas)—opportunities to be grasped *provided present staffing standards can be maintained*. As a whole the book attempts to counter the contraction in expectations of primary education and primary children which has developed among politicians, many parents and some teachers. Whilst rejecting world-shattering, society-reforming claims for education, contributors do attempt to raise expectations beyond a concern for the 'basics' (as these are usually defined). Thus for example, David Oliver and Robert Dearden argue that primary schools should be developing children's critical awareness of subjects such as history and mathematics; Mike Hill believes in introducing children to 'the fundamental interests of civilised life'; Joan Sallis and Bev. Woodruffe believe that schools can, and should, play a part (though only a part) in combating social and cultural disadvantage. All would agree with Alan Blyth that primary education should be regarded as appropriately 'primary' not as 'elementary education on top of which secondary education can be piled, as though it were a separate package containing rather more valuable goods' (page 134). Primary schools may seem far-removed from the wealth-producing sectors of our society (recently much beloved of politicians) but they are significant in both individual and social terms and not just because of their contribution in providing basic competencies.

Ten years ago *diversity* was a dominant theme in education. New institutions (such as Schools Council, teachers' centres and middle schools) were established; new schools were built to a startling variety of designs; different ways of organising time, staff, children and teaching spaces were advocated; attempts were made to diversify the primary curriculum. At present, greater *consistency* and *coherence* of policy and practice are urged on us. There has for example been talk of 'acceptable and unacceptable diversity' and of 'unacceptable differences from school to school in the content and quality of children's learning'. In the 1977 Green Paper gross inconsistencies in the quality of teaching received by children have been seen as requiring to be remedied. The primary survey reveals considerable inconsistencies in the coverage of essential elements and argues for ways of providing more consistent coverage in the primary curriculum.

To some extent this book shares the current concern for greater consistency and coherence in policy and practice. Though having very different philosophies of education both Mike Hill and David Oliver argue for coherent, consistent policies at school-level and spell out the nature of their policies; Norman Thomas advocates greater inter-school liaison to foster better curriculum consistency and continuity; Wynne Harlen is concerned at inconsistencies in teachers' attitudes towards, and treatment of, different areas of the curriculum; Joan Dean argues for common ground to be created within schools through staff discussion, schemes and check-lists as well as better liaison among schools to ensure the continuity and consistency of children's education: Derek Sharples wants a better coordinated, consistent policy for primary teacher education instead of the policy vacuum at present existing. What is being argued for is *not* uniformity of treatment, provision, policy or practice but in George Cooke's words 'some sort of balance between catering for difference and exploiting the common ground' (page 92). This is nowhere better illustrated than by Bev. Woodroffe's portrayal of the delicate issues involved in creating a policy for multicultural education. It would seem that concern for greater coherence and consistency both of policy and practice need not be at the expense of at least some of the diversity long cherished by many of us working in primary education.

The '60s and very early '70s were characterised by the advocacy of wide-scale educational *reform*. It was argued that curricula, institutional structures, teaching methods, forms of organisation and methods of assessment all needed radical reform in the light of social/economic changes and because of new knowledge. Primary schools were not exempt from this pressure for change: indeed it was claimed that as a result of the 'primary school revolution' they were in the vanguard of developments. Ten years on, claims for the reform movement in general and the 'revolutionised' English primary school in particular are more muted. Changes are seen to have taken place in some schools, major changes in a minority, but not on the national scale suggested by the myths. What is now being stressed is the need for careful *appraisal* of current policy and practice rather than the unquestioned challenge of past practice and the uncritical advocacy of innovation. The Bullock report, the Auld inquiry into William Tyndale Junior School, the 'Great Debate', the work of the APU and the national primary survey are all instances of appraisal.

This book is intended as a careful but frank contribution to the process of professional appraisal which is underway. It does not indulge in self-congratulation nor its opposite—both would be inappropriate responses to the crisis of confidence within and without the teaching profession. Successes are noted, improvements recognised, progress detected, but deficiencies are revealed, shortcomings analysed and policies suggested. The primary curriculum, the recommendations of the Warnock report, the school and the community, teacher education and the changing context of primary education are all subject to balanced professional appraisal. The need for institutional- and self-appraisal comes over strongly as does the necessity for teacher development rather than curriculum development or organisational change—a point particularly stressed by Leonard Marsh in the concluding chapter.

In his chapter on teacher development Derek Sharples makes much of the notions of 'competence' and 'judgment'. Both have always been needed in the difficult, complex and unpredictable task of educating young children; both are needed (even more) in the difficult, complex and unpredictable future facing us. This book hopes to make a modest but valuable contribution to enhancing the competence and judgment of policy-makers and practitioners in primary education.

Colin Richards

Contributors

Alan Blyth is Sydney Jones Professor of Education at the University of Liverpool. His publications include *English Primary Education* and (with Ray Derricott) *The Social Significance of Middle Schools*.

Howard Collings is Chief Statistician at the Department of Education and Science.

George Cooke is General Secretary, Society of Education Officers, and was formerly County Education Officer, Lincolnshire, and Vice-Chairman of the Warnock Committee.

Joan Dean is Chief Inspector for Surrey where she leads a team of inspectors who provide a monitoring and support service for the local authority and its teachers.

Robert Dearden is Professor of Education at the University of Birmingham Faculty of Education. He specialises in the philosophy of education and has a particular interest in primary education. His publications include *The Philosophy of Primary Education* and *Problems in Primary Education*.

Wynne Harlen is Senior Research Fellow, Chelsea College, and Deputy Director, Assessment of Performance in Science Project.

Mike Hill is headteacher of Terriers County Middle School, Buckinghamshire.

Tom Marjoram is Divisional Inspector for the Metropolitan and South Midlands Division and was until recently Head of the Assessment of Performance Unit.

Leonard Marsh is Principal, Bishop Grosseteste College, Lincoln, and Tutor responsible for a course for headteachers and others with special responsibilities in primary education.

David Oliver is headteacher of Evesham Church of England First School and Schoolmaster Fellow, Worcester College of Higher Education.

Colin Richards is Lecturer in Education, University of Leicester. He is editor of *Education 3–13,* joint general editor of *Educational Analysis* and honorary editor of the Association for the Study of the Curriculum.

Joan Sallis is 'a full-time parent' and was a parent member on the Taylor Committee.

Christopher Saville is Senior Schools Adviser for Suffolk County Council and has a particular interest in the primary and middle years of schooling.

Derek Sharples is Head of School and Dean of Education and Teaching Studies at Worcester College of Higher Education, where he is responsible for the initial and in-service education of teachers.

Roy Storrs is Primary Education Adviser for Shropshire where half of the primary schools have less than a hundred on the roll. He has a particular concern for and interest in the problems of small schools.

Norman Thomas is Chief Inspector for Primary Education, including nursery and middle schools. He is responsible for the general direction of the work of HMIs in primary education and, through the Senior Chief Inspector, for advising the Secretary of State and the DES on matters related to primary schools.

Bev. Woodroffe is ILEA Senior Inspector for Multi-Ethnic Education and Community Relations and is a member of the Community Relations Commission.

THE PRIMARY CURRICULUM

1

The Primary Curriculum:
survey findings and implications

Norman Thomas

Introduction

Throughout this chapter I shall use the word *curriculum* to mean those things that teachers plan that children shall learn, and learn to be. This is a narrower definition of the word than is sometimes used and excludes important things that children learn casually whether at home, in the street, or even at school. On the other hand, it is not intended to exclude relevant but unexpected bits of information that are brought to light as a piece of work goes forward; as, for example, when finding a disused mould for a keystone led children investigating an old brickfield to measure by how much the local clay shrank between being dug up and being taken from the kiln.

The methods that teachers use and the deployment of children and teachers are important in ensuring that learning takes place but they are not, except transiently, a part of what is to be learnt. The assumption will be made here that the methods and organisation used, including the ways in which the time is divided and labelled, are to be settled as a result of considering what is to be taught, the nature of the children, and the resources available, particularly the strengths of the teachers.

There are two other things to say by way of introduction. Discussion about the primary school curriculum has sometimes been presented as though it can be decided solely by reference to what is to be taught (the subject-centred curriculum), or solely by reference to children's interests, abilities or a combination of characteristics. In practice, both subject matter and children have to be considered when planning curricula. What is to be included ought to be worth learning at least for the present and often for the future; and the children must already know enough and be sufficiently motivated to be able to grasp what they are expected to learn. The last introductory point seems, nowadays, so obvious that it might be thought hardly worth making. No two schools have precisely the same resources or the same environment. Inevitably, there are differences in the curriculum from school to school. Equally, and in some particularly important ways, there is a degree of uniformity. The debate about uniformity that has been going on for some years now is a debate about degree, not about absolutes.

Three chapters out of eight in *Primary Education in England* (1978) deal with the curriculum. Chapter 4 considers planning and continuity; Chapter 5 deals with the content of the curriculum, and Chapter 6 with scope and with standards as judged by a consideration of what was being taught (whether the work was matched at about the right level of difficulty for the children, or too easy, or too difficult) and the results of objective tests in reading and mathematics for 11 year olds and in reading for 9 year olds. Content, scope and match were judged by HMI on the basis of observation in classrooms.

Additionally, Annex B, which summarises the schedules used by HMIs in making their returns, outlines the curricular activities that were noted. This annex also lists the various resources that provided starting points for the work in hand: books, television and radio, assignment cards and the local environment as well as direct stimulation from the teacher. The fact that the schedules used were the same for classes with 7, 9 or 11 year olds—the three age groups included in the survey—makes it possible to say with some confidence how curricula changed as children matured.

The Basic Skills

In only one respect does the survey have anything to say about whether schools were better, the same or worse than in earlier years. The NS6 reading test, administered by the National Foundation for Educational Research (NFER), consists of 60 sentences each with a word missing. About 5000 randomly chosen children from the randomly selected schools and classes were asked to choose which of a number of given words should fill the gaps. The results of the 1976/77 survey and of the surveys of 1955, 1960 and 1970, when the same test was used, are displayed in the report of the main survey. It is sufficient to indicate here that the results of the four surveys are consistent with gradually improving standards over the period covered.

Although doubt has been expressed from time to time about reading standards in primary schools, the findings of the survey are not surprising—though they are encouraging—when considered against the account of what is done in schools. There is ample evidence to show that primary school teachers give very high priority to teaching children how to read. All classes with 7 or 9 year olds made use of graded reading schemes; 85 per cent of the schools had schemes of work on language, a percentage exceeded only for mathematics. What is more, reading material was more likely to be appropriately matched in difficulty to the ability of the children than was the level of work in any other aspect of the curriculum; this was true for 7, 9 and 11 year olds and for the average, more able and less able children as identified within each class by the class teacher. The match was best for the less able children and least good for the more able children, a pattern common to each aspect of the curriculum on which a judgment was made.

5

Paragraph 6.5 of the report lists the separate curricular items found to be included in the work of 80 per cent or more of classes. So far as reading was concerned, the items identified were:

a (in 7 and 9 year old classes) children practised reading from a main reading scheme and from supplementary readers;
b (in 9 and 11 year old classes) children read fiction and non-fiction which was not related to other work they were doing in the classroom;
c (in 11 year old classes) children made use of information books related to work in other areas of the curriculum;
d (at each age) children were encouraged to select books of their own choice.

Comparison with Annex B shows that the following items fell below that level of frequency:

a the use of extended reading skills;
b children's comments on the materials read;
c the reading of poetry by children;
d children's discussion of books at more than a superficial level.

Furthermore, children in only about two-fifths of the 7 and 9 year old classes and in half the 11 year old classes appeared to turn readily and naturally to books for pleasure during the course of the day. The children in rather fewer classes appeared to use books with ease and confidence as a source of information. While there were opportunities for children to select books for themselves in almost all classes, these opportunities could usefully have been increased in more than three-fifths of the classes.

These findings give some clues about what needs to be done if the more able and the average are to be taken further. The report, having acknowledged the hard work teachers do to ensure that the elementary skills are acquired, spells out some of the implications in paragraph 5.47. Once the skills of decoding are firmly established further skills should be introduced: these include using dictionaries and reference books efficiently, skimming passages for quick retrieval of information, scanning passages to establish the main points, interpreting context clues and being able to make sense of difficult passages.

It is pointed out in Chapter 8 that for this to be achieved 'children need to be introduced to a wide range of reading material in connection with many aspects of their work'. That thought is carried further in paragraph 8.28. This points out that the children in classes which covered a full range of the widely taught items did better on the NFER tests at 9 and 11 years of age; and, for all three age groups, the work of the children in these classes was better matched to their abilities than was the work of children in other classes. It has to be remembered that the widely taught items covered social studies and aesthetics as well as language, literacy and mathematics. It would be tedious to go through each aspect of the curriculum merely to demonstrate that what can be said about reading can be said, in some form, about the others. The general message is clear: the elementary work is thoroughly done, but the average and particularly the more able children could go further. The particular message, however, is not quite the same for each part of the curriculum.

It was observed that in virtually all classes children undertook some form of narrative writing, for example, relating stories, recounting adventures from real life or fantasy or describing their own experiences. In very few were children presented with a writing task which involved presenting a coherent argument, exploring alternative possibilities or drawing conclusions and making judgments. Of course, this is a difficult form of writing for young children, but it could have been more regularly encouraged among the older and abler children.

Taken together, the HMI observations and the NFER test for 11 year olds show quite clearly that children practised the

7

basic skills in arithmetic and that considerable attention was paid to computation, measurement and calculations involving sums of money. The results of this practice were disappointing, particularly in two respects. Children of 6 and 7 onwards have practice in reading block graphs and the NFER test showed that nearly all 11 year old children could read block graphs, but only 28 per cent managed to read a fairly simple line graph. Equally important, the strenuous efforts of teachers, teacher trainers, advisers and inspectors over recent years have still left 40 per cent or so of 11 year olds unable to say which of the four rules of number, applied to a given pair of numbers, will produce the smallest answer.

Children who were taught from the blackboard and also did practical work in connection with number scored particularly well on the NFER test. This may seem to have more implications for method than for the curriculum, but perhaps the underlying points are that the children need to be able to apply what they learn in a variety of circumstances and also the chance to develop a working understanding of the various processes they use. Neither may occur if each assignment and each sum is treated as a separate piece of experience.

Social Studies and Religious Education

In some ways the most interesting implications in the survey relate to history and geography. One of the greatest changes that has taken place in primary schools over the past two decades is the development of topic work in place of the separate study of history and of geography through textbooks written for the purpose. The textbooks formerly in use were often very thin in content and all too frequently based on out of date material. We should not gain by returning to them. Two arguments frequently advanced in favour of the topic approach are first, that the topic can be chosen to suit the children's interests and second, that the topic approach overcomes the harmful fragmentation of work that may happen at the primary school level when each subject is taught separately.

What the survey seems to have uncovered is that the topic approach may itself produce another kind of fragmentation: the divorce of one topic from the next. What is called for is a better definition of the ideas, the skills and the techniques that children might learn during their primary school years so that each topic can be chosen and arranged to contribute to the development of these. Some topics now undertaken may not be best suited to such purposes, but there is no reason why the alternative content chosen should be any less interesting than at present.

The content chosen for any single topic has also to be considered in relation to the rest of the programme. Any one topic may contain religious, historical, geographical or other material, and each kind may reinforce the rest. In the programme as a whole, it is important to be sure that each subject is properly represented either in combination or separately, and that the ideas, attitudes and skills appropriate to each are suitably developed. Religious education requires special consideration partly because teachers sometimes find it particularly necessary to make the religious implications of the material explicit for children and partly because children now in our schools come from a much wider range of religious and cultural backgrounds than formerly.

What has been said about the development of reading, writing and mathematics, and particularly about the need to apply the skills involved in these subjects to other matter, has particular relevance for the work in history and geography. The question of whether the topic chosen will contribute to the development of basic skills, as most will, is another criterion that might be borne in mind when making a choice. Of course, such hopes for development and extension will come to little if, as too often happens, the topic leads merely to children copying material from a reference book into an exercise book.

9

Art and Craft

The importance of the underlying skills and techniques is also clear in connection with art and craft. But in these subjects an additional skill to be fostered is that of observing carefully. Superb examples of children's work are reproduced in *Art in Junior Education* (1978). These can leave no one in doubt of the potential of some children in primary schools when they are taught to use their eyes and to use material and techniques effectively.

Science

In the science schedule no items, or combination of associated items, were found being taught in as many as 80 per cent of the classes of any of the three age groups. The schedules covered a range of possible content and allowed for noting occasions when children recorded observations, thought about what they had seen or otherwise experienced, came to some view why things might be as they were, and then conducted simple tests to examine the validity of their view. Why is the grass yellow under the loose paving stone? Is it because the paving stone is heavy? Or because the paving stone is made of concrete? Or is it because the light cannot get to the grass? Or is it because the rain cannot get to it? How can we find out which of these is probably true?

The kind of science being considered in the HMI primary survey was much more to do with children observing and thinking than with children using bunsen burners. It was not particularly physical science as against biological. The difficulty that primary school teachers have had in taking on and adapting the various primary science projects of the last two decades suggests that teachers in general are not convinced of the worth of this kind of work, or that they find it extremely difficult to organise, or that they feel too unsure of themselves to undertake it. It may be that all three reasons play a part. Yet the work that does take place in some schools shows what can be done and how much children can gain from it.

Music, Physical Education and Posts of Curricular Responsibility

It is open to question whether it is reasonable to expect teachers to take on the suggestions made in this chapter in addition to what they do at present. The answer from the survey must be that it is not reasonable unless additional support is given to class teachers. But where can that support come from?

The work in music and physical education came out relatively well in the way that it was matched to children's abilities, almost as well as in mathematics and reading. Both were notable because so many schools had teachers with special responsibilities for them; indeed there was a music specialist in 70 per cent of the schools, more than for any other named area of curricular responsibility. Environmental studies and science were each covered by teachers with special responsibility in only 17 per cent of schools and even language, including reading, and mathematics were listed in only 51 per cent and 45 per cent respectively.

Further evidence that teachers with posts of special responsibility can be vitally important is shown in Notes 12a, b and c of the report. In the minority of schools where teachers with posts of responsibility have a strong influence there is a far greater likelihood that the work is better matched to the children's abilities at each level of ability within a class.

The use of teachers' strengths beyond their own classrooms cannot be effective if it depends only on casual staffroom meetings. Teachers with curricular responsibilities need to be thought of as part of the in-service training provision; they should be responsible for producing guidelines and schemes of work; for organising in-school courses (sometimes with

11

help from outside); and they should also acquire firsthand experience of what is happening in other classes in the school so that the most apt form of assistance can be given to fellow members of staff. Sometimes, but unusually for as long as a year and with a whole class, it may be necessary for the teacher with special responsibility to take on the direct teaching of some children. These children are more likely than not to be the slowest or the more able children, and the older more often than the younger ones. The exercise of these responsibilities needs to be accompanied by a strengthening of the rôle of the class teacher. The latter should continue to be responsible for the whole range of work of the class and call in the curricular specialist just as he or she might use a television programme, a teachers' manual, a local authority adviser or a college of education lecturer.

What is envisaged is a far cry from the traditional specialist practices in secondary schools. It is assumed that even 11 year olds will, for the most part, be taught by their class teacher. However, each week or so arrangements will be made between teachers, with the head's agreement, so that the best use can be made of their individual talents. Those talents may be called upon in advising on the direction a piece of work might now take, on how it might be tackled, or directly in the business of teaching.

Interrelations between Parts of the Curriculum

Although the curriculum has been discussed so far in terms of separate activities or subjects, it has been a recurring theme that work in one subject may influence and extend work in another. A simple example happened when a teacher was planning a study of the different characteristics of various brands of washing-up liquid. She could, from the point of view of the science she wanted to do, simply have persuaded the children to stir the various liquids under identical conditions and then to measure the amount of froth produced. That would inevitably have produced yet more block graphs. Instead, she prepared for measuring the amount of froth in each case at regular intervals and plotting the way in which the froth developed, so producing the material for a series of line graphs. But it is extremely difficult to consider the interrelations between the various parts of the curriculum unless one has some overview of what it should contain.

For the purposes of the HMI primary survey the curriculum was divided into five parts: language and literacy; mathematics; science; aesthetics, and social studies. There was no supposition that any one of those elements must appear as such on the time-table, though it is common to find that some do. The more common curricular divisions twenty-five years ago were given a series of subject or skills titles and were to be found on time-tables: English, reading, geography, and so on. More recently time-tables have been blocked—sometimes by the class teacher rather than the head—but there has still been much less carry-over from one part of the time-table to another than is sometimes supposed. One effect has been the reluctance of a substantial number of teachers to deal with the suitability of the English used during topic work and another the enclosure of mathematics within its own time-tabled periods.

Perhaps it is not enough to lay a single grid across the curriculum for the purpose of analysing it. Any of those referred to above—survey areas, subjects, time-table dimensions—might, in some circumstances, be of some use. Whichever is used, it might also be productive to analyse the whole curriculum from these four points of view: the range and selection of content; the skills to be learnt; the ideas to be acquired and developed; and the attitudes to be fostered. The opportunities that could come from a cross-check of this sort could lead to a more useful concept of balance in the curriculum than discussions that start from thoughts about whether environmental studies should be given one or two hours a week.

13

Content, Skills, Ideas and Attitudes

The content of the work must range across the way people have lived in the past and live now—and live in the minds of writers and film-makers. It must allow children to come to terms with other living things and the material world. Selection needs to take account of children's present knowledge and likely interests as well as adult judgments about what is worth knowing.

The skills need to include not only skills of language and mathematics but also those of observing (including measuring and weighing) and of creating and making, whether through art, crafts, music or dance.

Particular ideas that need to be acquired are far too numerous to develop here but many of them are variations on the power to discriminate, the ability to abstract and generalise and the ability to perceive interrelations. The ability to understand and use symbols is vital to most parts of the curriculum and not least to language and mathematics.

Perhaps the most important thing to say about attitudes is that none will do for every circumstance. While children should be taught to persist, as they must be, they should also be taught to adapt. While they should be taught to be independent, they must also be taught to cooperate.

A clearer identification of the skills, ideas and attitudes that should be included in a curriculum may further underline the importance of careful, even frugal, selection of content. It may be that fewer topics should be attempted, but that each should be used more thoroughly to advance the children's thinking, feeling and skills. It is not sensible to suppose that any individual teacher or head can be responsible for planning the whole curriculum. Even a staff of eight or more cannot, sensibly, in isolation, make the decisions necessary. Contact with other schools in the neighbourhood and current thinking about what is important is essential if there is to be a sufficient fit between phases of schooling. The children's lives are continuous even if schooling is not.

In identifying what should be included in the curriculum it is sensible to consider what is now common. The curricular items in paragraph 6.5 of the report, and referred to earlier in this chapter, give a starting list. Thought needs to be given to whether the list contains some items that do not merit a place or, and this is the more likely, is lacking in some necessary particulars. Should not, for example, all the classes with 9 year olds include estimation and measurement of length; and provide for children to learn, at first hand, to respect and care for living things?

Of course, schools in a locality should be able to produce their own list of commonly taught items as a basis for discussion between schools, primary and secondary, about the curriculum. To do so would be to provide a positive basis for development rather than, as happens all too often, discussion that starts from a melancholy regret about what appears to be missing.

Contracting Rolls and Small Schools

In schools with fewer than 8–10 teachers there may be real problems in covering the range of work that needs to be done both in planning and in implementation [as Roy Storrs argues in Chapter 14]. Some small schools are already combining forces in such a way that joint discussion and planning take place (pages 167–8). In some cases, teachers from one school give occasional help in another. The effect of falling rolls on the sizes of primary schools is described in Chapter 13 and there can be no doubt that many more schools than now might benefit from the above arrangements during the next decade.

It is easy to see that if a teacher in a secondary school is not replaced because the school roll has fallen seriously, then a whole subject may have to be left out of the curriculum for some pupils. What is not so apparent is that in primary schools the loss of expertise when one teacher in the group leaves

15

may, if that expertise is lost, lead to a deterioration in the quality of what is done in all classes.

Falling rolls may also increase the number of classes of 26 and more children with a mixture of age groups. The HMI primary survey indicates that the performance of children in these classes is likely, on average, to be less good than that of children in single-age classes unless special counterbalancing measures are taken. So far as the curriculum is concerned one problem is to ensure that children in mixed age classes engage in as many of the widely taught items as is common in single-age classes.

Of course, there are potential gains to be had from falling rolls if teachers are helped to secure them. If present staffing standards can be maintained in a system with a larger proportion of small schools than now, the average size of classes is likely to be smaller and pupil-teacher ratios more favourable overall. There will almost certainly be more space per child even if the least suitable or the temporary accommodation now in use is discarded.

Benefits are there for the taking but they require a clear view of what is to be taught. They call for both the continuation of the present sound policies that lead children to acquire the elementary skills, and some changes of expectation and practice of the kind referred to in this chapter. It would be a great pity if this period of contracting numbers was thought of only as a period of difficulties; the opportunity for improving service to children is there, and so is the chance to make the job of teaching in primary schools still more satisfying.

References

Department of Education and Science, 1978, *Art in Junior Education,* London, HMSO

Department of Education and Science, 1978, *Primary Education in England: A Survey by HM Inspectors of Schools,* London, HMSO

2

The Primary Survey:
an assessment

Robert Dearden

First impressions of the Inspectorate's report on primary
education may be false ones. For example, in December 1978
the editorial in *Child Education* said that 'It is hard to know what
to make of the Inspectorate's report on *Primary Education in
England . . .* really the trouble with the report as a whole [is that]
it's not anything much'. A generous way of accounting for this
unfavourable impression would be to see it as an indirect tribute
to Plowden. For the Plowden Report of 1967 set new high
standards. It was comprehensive. It constantly interwove
theory and practice. It had memorable keynote passages, such as
the one containing the assertion that 'the child is the agent in his
own learning'. This latest report, by contrast, is intentionally
limited in scope, and it contains neither any explicit theory nor
any purple passages. One way of seeing it as related to Plowden,
however, is to see it as a response to Plowden's call (para. 290)
for surveys of the quality of primary education to be undertaken
every ten years. But if by such 'quality' was intended a
confirmation of the spread of Plowden's own child-centred
philosophy, then this latest report cannot be seen as such a
confirmation, for reasons that will soon be apparent.

Of all people, the Inspectorate are in the best position to
report on the schools as a whole. Not only do they as a body
cover the whole country, but they can also rely on co-operation,
as we see in the 99.6 per cent response rate to the headteachers'
long questionnaire (a response rate to my knowledge matched

17

only by Soviet elections). Their first and most obvious finding is of very great political importance. This is that the schools have not 'abandoned the basics', standards are not falling (except that of HMI's spelling in the first printing), every other school is not a Tyndale and chaos does not reign. The angry censure to which primary schools have recently been subjected, and the wild and evidently baseless accusations that have been thrown at them by some parents, by the press and by some politicians, can now be confidently turned aside. There is no need to 'get back to the basics' and indeed schools do better if they pursue the basics through a wide curriculum. In fact, an opposite problem now looming up will be to protect the width of the curriculum in the face of contracting rolls and staff.

Then are there grounds for complacency? Apparently there are grounds for satisfaction where the less able 50 per cent of pupils are concerned [as Chapter 1 points out]. The work being done with these children is broadly as it should be. But the position with the more able is rather more disconcerting. With these children there is indeed a problem. And it is not just the problem which Plowden thought might exist of adequately stretching the 'gifted', or the most able 5 per cent. The report finds that the more able 50 per cent are not being sufficiently stretched. Their work is superficial, is not challenging, and it lacks progression. Two general statements of this deficiency are the following:

8.33 *the more able children within a class were the least likely to be doing work that was sufficiently challenging* (their italics)
8.67 the immediate aim . . . should probably be to take what is done to greater depth rather than to introduce content that is new to primary education.

Hints of a need for some intellectual stiffening regularly appear. Thus 'more could be done . . . to encourage them to follow a line of argument, to evaluate evidence, or to reach judgements in the course of discussion'.

This general deficiency is particularised. Thus the report

18

urges attention to advanced reading skills such as scanning, skimming, interpreting, seeing implications and following arguments critically. More difficult writing tasks are advocated such as presenting a coherent argument, exploring alternative possibilities, drawing conclusions and making judgments. In mathematics, more demanding work should be set rather than further repetitive practice. Science should go beyond the present superficial level to more careful observation and accurate recording, the formulation of hypotheses and the testing of them. History should go beyond superficial copying from reference books and lead towards an understanding of historical change and an awareness of the nature of historical evidence. Similarly, geography should go beyond superficial weather observations.

Earlier I remarked that this report is not just a confirmation of the spread of 'quality' understood in the Plowden sense. A significantly different educational philosophy is implicitly contained in these suggestions. Let part of paragraph 544 in Plowden serve as a reminder of what was sought in 1967:

> 'The newer methods start with the direct impact of the environment on the child and the child's individual response to it. The results are unpredictable but extremely worthwhile. The teacher has to be prepared to follow up the personal interest of the children who, either singly, or in groups, follow divergent paths of discovery. . . . The teacher needs perception to appreciate the value of what can be gained from this method of working, and he needs also energy to keep up with the children's demands.'

Thus the Plowden stress was on 'spontaneous' interests, discovery, and following the lead of the child.

Now contrast some statements from the 1978 report:

8.25 *Curricular content should be selected not only to suit the interests and abilities of the children and to provide for the progressive development of the basic skills, but also because it*

19

> *is important in its own right.* . . . . The teacher's need for a thorough knowledge of the subject becomes more marked as the children get older (their italics).

8.58 It is vital that teachers should be knowledgeable in what they teach.

Here and elsewhere in the report the emphasis is un-Plowdenlike. The importance of an ordered and progressive curriculum is assumed. There is to be the teaching of groups round a blackboard. Special posts for curricular areas are recommended and special curricular strengths of staff are to be exploited. As rolls contract, freed rooms are seen in terms of possible specialist purposes. Although specialist teaching on the secondary school model is not advocated, there is the unmistakable impression of thinking from secondary practices downwards rather than, as with Plowden, thinking from infant school practices upwards.

This is not the place to raise once again the merits of the Plowden philosophy. That is something which has been considered in detail and at length elsewhere (Peters 1969, *Education 3–13*, 1978). The context in which the latest report places its change in philosophy is one of social demands for rising levels of skill. Such a utilitarian conception, valid though it is, is not the only conception which might be invoked. Surely doing greater justice to intellectual development can be justified also in terms of individual fulfilment and the realisation of worthwhile individual powers and abilities? The more able children deserve to be stretched quite apart from social utility. It may not be much use to an employer if attention has been given to historical change and evidence, or if in geography the work went beyond simple weather observations, but such things are very relevant to leading a more interesting and fully engaged life. In short, something of the intentions behind the idea of a liberal education can be appropriately invoked, though admittedly they may lack political cutting edge where narrow counsels prevail. Nevertheless, it is important that educators should not forget what they are about, even if less generous conceptions have to be relied upon in speaking to the world at large.

I shall not comment further on the question of the general justification for this implicit shift away from a Plowden philosophy, beyond venturing the opinion that in my view the report is justified where junior and middle schools are concerned, in trying to effect such a shift. There is, however, another matter that calls for comment. In spite of its insistence that greater attention should be given to the intellectual development of the 50 per cent or so of more able children, the report is really rather vague about what form that intellectual development should take. Perhaps it was the proper task of the report to do no more than to raise the level of awareness of this problem, leaving to others and to other sorts of occasion the working out of how the problem might be solved. Such a report admittedly cannot do everything itself, but must be supplemented by local action in the way of sensitising conferences, in-service courses, advisory programmes, exchange visits between schools and so on. But even at its chosen level of generality, does the report rightly conceptualise the problem? How, indeed, does it conceptualise it?

To judge from the passages quoted earlier in juxtaposition to some passages from Plowden, it might be thought that a greater emphasis on intellectual development would mean giving more attention to the traditional range of curricular *subjects*. The children, and presumably also their teachers, should simply learn more about and deepen their understanding of the usual range of subjects. There are passages which do suggest that this was what was meant, and it seems intelligible and defensible enough. Thus the report comments on the inadequacy of teaching children graphical methods of representing data only to the extent of teaching them how to construct simple block graphs and then being content endlessly to vary that one theme. What more, then, might be wanted? Suggestions are readily conceivable. For example, the connection with averages can be noted, and how the blocks above the average line equal the spaces below it. Line graphs can be introduced and the characteristic discussed that every point on the line must have significance, so making it necessary to choose appropriately the form of graph to employ. Axes can be extended to negative values. Misleading graphical displays, culled perhaps from newspapers, can be discussed. Circular displays can be introduced, linking the work with percentages and angular measure . . . and so on.

To take another example, the report says that historical work is deficient in that no attention is given to historical change and the nature of historical evidence. Is that an inappropriate secondary school conception? A primary teacher might, for example, duplicate copies of some pages of an early local census return to serve as evidence. On that basis, such changes might be discussed as fashions in Christian names, size of family, kinds of work, wives and work, schooling ages and geographical mobility. Links with other subjects (something much advocated in the report) might be sought through the use of maps, associated computations and the introduction of the idea of a possible sampling error in generalising from such limited evidence. In ways such as these, greater intellectual development can be seen to involve not just more information but critical attention to evidence, discussion of its possible significance or interpretation, and setting the matter in a wider context of understanding. In these and other ways the older and more able children can begin more fully to enter into the possession of their potential intellectual powers.

For suggestions such as these to be practicable, it may well be that secondary practice should be copied at least to the extent of allowing primary teachers more free time for the preparation and following up of work in the classroom. This is one possibility presented by contracting rolls which the report does not much discuss, though at some future time people may well look back and wonder how teachers were ever expected to sustain such a highly professional level of imaginative activity throughout a whole day without breaks for planning, preparation of materials, collecting data and the like. But such practical difficulties apart, the work envisaged would at least be acceptably conceptualised.

There is, however, an alternative conception which regularly surfaces throughout the report. In this conception, intellectual development is thought of as a developing of certain apparently quite general *skills*. For example, there is a whole section entitled 'learning to notice and to think' (5.10–5.13). In that section, children are envisaged as 'learning to notice relevant features'. Elsewhere, a new basic skill makes its appearance, namely 'comprehension' (6.5), and children are to be taught 'to comprehend the main ideas in information given to them'. At 5.21, 'listening skills' appear and at 5.47 reading skills such as 'the capacity to make sense of difficult passages'. At 5.72, we are urged to 'teach children how to make careful observations', because 'in science it is essential that children should develop observational skills and begin to recognise similarities and differences' (5.70). 'Observing skill' is returned to in the final chapter where it is said that '*Intending primary school teachers should be helped to recognise the importance of teaching children to observe carefully, encouraging them to try to explain what they have noticed and to test their explanations*' (8.56, their italics).

This conception of intellectual development is, to put it mildly, highly controversial. In the philosophy of education it is debated under the title 'general powers of the mind', the question at issue being whether there can be such *general* powers (Brown 1975). Can there be such general skills as skill in noticing, observing skill, thinking skill, comprehension skill or listening skill? If there cannot be, then effort will be misdirected in trying to improve primary education in pursuit of such skills and related in-service training will be wrongly focused. The question is therefore no 'merely academic' one, or a matter 'just of semantics'. The question has a long history which goes back to faculty psychology and the idea that certain subjects, such as Latin, could train the general mental powers and so make us fit for any specific future task. Reasoning, memory, judgment, imagination, will and observation each had its appropriate muscle-developing exercises.

Certainly there can be skills of general application. It would be very surprising if this were not so, since otherwise why should we class activities together and call them by the same name? For example, across all the varieties of subject for discussion, there are some generally relevant observances, such as listening to what others say, contributing relevantly and separating oneself from the substance of the view put forward for discussion. But such skills (if skill is the right word) will not be sufficient for the discussion to be a good one, since for that to happen the participants must also be knowledgeable in the subject matter under discussion. The same point could be made about a supposed general 'interviewing skill' of the sort that television trainees might be given. There would indeed be common elements of skill in approaching inter-viewees, but also needed would be some specific knowledge of the subject matter of the interview. So commonly is this lacking that in practice we all too often witness fatuous questions, or no capacity to follow up a reply, or no awareness of standard objections to what is said. The general skills are not sufficient.

The same points can be made about the report's supposed general skills. There may indeed be something in common to all occasions of listening (paying attention for example) but specific knowledge is needed if we are to listen to (or for) the reed-warbler, the wrong engine valve-setting, the rhythm of the poetic line, the minor key, the Frenchman's message, the scientific explanation or the note of regret. 'General listening skill', if there is such a thing, would be rather trivial by comparison with specifics here. Much the same goes for general 'observing skill'. What we observe is relative to our knowledge and interests. The sharpest of hedgerow observers may still fail to notice that his wife has had her hair done, and the keenest follower of the detail design differences in the latest marks of cars may be blind to pattern in the landscape. Much the same points would need to be made about any supposed general 'thinking skill' or 'problem-solving skill'. And what on earth is a general (or 'basic') comprehension skill supposed to consist of? Where there is generality, then let us by all means draw attention to it and so anticipate whole classes of future experiences; but at the same time let us also recognise that 'skills' can become a mindless incantation serving only to render vague what we should be seeking to teach.

Two powerful pressures push towards the 'general skills' conception of intellectual development, though mistakenly. These are the explosion in knowledge and the obsolescence of knowledge. There is too much knowledge and what we learn of it may cease to be useful. If we could find some more economically learned and more permanently valuable general skills, then they would indeed constitute golden knowledge . . . if such skills existed. Certainly some accommodation to these pressures is possible. We can teach children how to find out what they do not know (provided that this source of information will be comprehensible when it is located). We can teach the methodology of a subject, where there is one. And the particular can be milked of as much generality as it will yield. But in order to see that all of this will fall far short of the dream, consider a supposed general teaching skill. Rather than train teachers to teach mathematics, or art, or physical education, or music, or religion, or biology, should we instead go for 'general teaching skill'? There would indeed be something to learn, but would it be sufficient? Can a sixth form history teacher be put straight into a nursery class? Can a junior school teacher take over a university seminar on the Icelandic sagas or new techniques in dentistry?

I take the answers to be obvious. If by 'listening skill' is meant no more than that children should pay attention when their teachers explain something, or if by 'observing skill' is meant noticing certain particular sorts of feature to which in

25

one way or another attention is drawn, then there is no objection. Something rather specific is then being referred to in a misleadingly over-general way. And the fault of the report here might arguably be no more than that. But I think a rather deeper misconception is at work, which makes important practical differences. For example, if the more able 50 per cent need only to acquire certain general skills, such as noticing skill, then in-service courses and other sorts of help for teachers will seem unnecessary. Just get the children to 'notice' more. But if the intellectual development sought is by way of, for example, a deepened understanding of science (which will of course include some specific *problem-related* observing, listening, comprehending etc.) then both teachers and taught will need to know or to learn some science.

What I have been suggesting about the latest HMI report is as follows. The report should perform a valuable political function in getting ill-informed and sensationalist critics off the backs of the primary schools. Where the less able half of primary children are concerned, the schools are doing well, as they are with all children in the elementary parts of the traditional basic subjects. But the report is not mere confirmation of the spread of Plowden's ideas. It somewhat departs from Plowden's child-centred philosophy more towards a subject-centred view. However, this departure is not a return to fact-cramming or the rote learning of blocks of information, but an advocacy of stimulating intellectual development. How is that to be conceived? Here the report is unclear as to what it wants, and unclear in ways which could compromise choosing the right targets for in-service help. My own suggestion is that intellectual development should be conceived as a deepening critical awareness of subjects along the lines earlier illustrated with reference to mathematics and history. The alternative conception as developing a set of quite general skills is largely a misconception, since even where there is such generality it is often trivial, and it is never sufficient.

References

Brown, S. (ed.), 1975, *Philosophers Discuss Education,* London, Macmillan, part two

Department of Education and Science, 1978, *Primary Education in England: A Survey by HM Inspectors of Schools,* London, HMSO

Education 3–13, 1978, Vol. 6 No. 1

Peters, R. (ed.), 1969, *Perspectives on Plowden,* London, Routledge and Kegan Paul

3

Assessment

Tom Marjoram

Introduction

In this 'Year of the Child' no one can deny that professional opinion has moved a long way from the days of children being 'seen and not heard', when 'silence was golden', to the present day when we like to think that we regard children in school primarily as individuals having widely differing strengths, weaknesses, characteristics and needs.

Back in 1870 it was a major achievement to provide children with schools and education of any kind but since then there have been progressively more sensitive attempts to match instruction to different ages, aptitudes and abilities. Thus pupil grouping has moved through successive stages of ability separation by 'standard', chronological separation by age, streaming within a whole year group to grouping within the class and/or withdrawal for special help—a trend which increasingly recognises that no group of children anywhere can be regarded as homogeneous.

The recent primary survey (1978) shows a good match between ability and provision for some children in all areas of the curriculum [as Norman Thomas indicates in Chapter 1]. This was very noticeable in the case of the less able children and especially in the case of the basic subjects, of PE and of music. However, the survey also reports that the ablest children within a class, whatever the actual range of ability, were often given work which was too easy for them. Where poorness of match occurred it tended to take the form, not of over-expectation, but of under-expectation. Many of the abler children could have been attempting harder, more complex, more interesting, more challenging work than they were actually being set.

If this is accepted—and it is difficult to dispute the extensive basis of evidence upon which this finding rests—then it is a serious matter. It cannot possibly be because teachers are too kind-hearted or because they do not earnestly attempt to do their best for the children. The reasons may be complex but in this chapter I shall argue that one of the most important is that some of our assessment procedures leave much to be desired.

Effective assessment is at the heart of good teaching and good management. It alone gives reliable feedback to guide us in our work. It takes many forms and serves many purposes. It can range from informal questioning and discussion through regular marking and spot testing to formal internal and external examinations. This diversity is well exemplified on a national scale by the different approaches used in the primary survey and by the APU.

The latter necessarily uses techniques which involve samples of 11, 13 and 15 year old pupils responding to test items. The responses are mainly written, though verbal responses are required in the practical mathematics and science surveys. Whatever mode is employed, the responses are scored and the surveys are designed in such a way as to identify trends and changes in performance levels. They will tell us some useful things but by no means all we wish to know about schools. On the other hand, the primary survey employed many other modes of assessment including systematic consideration of what was taught, examination of a very wide range of childrens' work, and a great deal of direct talking to children about their efforts. It inevitably produced a wealth of information and indirectly suggested to teachers ways of improving continuous and self assessment in their schools.

Assessment in school can serve many purposes. The most

29

common purpose is effected by mastery or criterion-referenced tests in which the teacher simply wishes to check that a child or group of children, or indeed the whole class, have acquired sufficient mastery of a topic to move on to the next one. Diagnostic testing is concerned with finding out the precise nature of a •difficulty which seems to be impeding learning or, on the other hand, with identifying a particular strength which is resulting in work of promise. Occasionally assessment is simply to compare group with group; to see how a particular class or school measures up to the national age group. For this purpose some kind of norm-referenced test is required.

Assessment, too, takes place at all *ages*. With young children it is bound to be largely based on observation and verbal communication and is very much a continuous process. As children grow older and become able to write, follow instructions, use tapes and so on, the means of assessment can become increasingly diversified though, of course, day by day observation continues to play a crucial part.

The *kinds* of assessment or measurements which are made in different subjects also vary widely. The technology of testing reading or basic skills in arithmetic is well advanced and proficiency is measurable upon fairly well defined linear scales. However, when an attempt is made to measure, for example, levels of reading comprehension, or the ability to generalise or innovate in mathematics, assessment becomes a more complex process. Indeed, in areas of personal and social development where critical faculties or expressive abilities are involved, assessment can become very complex—even controversial—and often a matter for the specialist teacher. Clear criteria in these areas may be difficult to discern and linear measurement inappropriate, undesirable or impossible.

Again, the so-called 'measurement' of attitudes is often not a matter of measurement but of description and circumstance. Take for instance 'perseverance'. This can range from unwillingness to try at all to a pig–headed refusal to stop trying under all circumstances. The optimum measure would depend upon attendant circumstances. It could be that the 'best' attitude usually is one of balance midway along the scale. In some circumstances, however, unbending adherence to sincerely held principles might deserve the highest merit—awards for gallantry are of this kind. Yet there are circumstances where odds are so great that any effort would be wasted and perseverance would be in vain.

One of the fears commonly voiced in the assessment of affective factors is that it is impossible to avoid making value judgments. Insofar as any assessment by its very selection and emphasis bears a value judgment this is true, but it needs to be strongly refuted that assessment in the aesthetic or personality fields necessarily labels certain attitudes as 'good' and others as 'bad'. Indeed, the best assessments simply display in objective detail the range of attitudes or preferences of a group and leave the reader to evaluate them. This said, it is my experience that robust attempts to assess even in these difficult fields nearly always have a beneficial effect upon standards of work. The object of most school assessment is to make helpful statements about ways in which a situation can be improved and this, after all, is why children go to school—to improve their performance—not just in the basic skills but in the whole range of the activities they experience there.

General Aspects of Assessment

In the primary survey Inspectors looked at very many aspects of primary school work and many of the recommendations made in Chapter 8 point strongly towards the need for sharper assessment. The scene is set in paragraph 8.58:

'It is vital that teachers should be knowledgeable in what they teach; it is just as necessary that they should be able to assess the performance of their pupils in terms of what they next need to be taught. The survey has shown that even

31

some experienced teachers find it difficult to judge the appropriate level of work.'

This and other more detailed recommendations come at a time when other circumstances make progress possible. Chapter 13 discusses how, during the 1980s, we shall see a continuing fall in the number of pupils in our schools and possibly also an improvement in staffing standards—though the latter remains to be seen. If it happened it would allow teachers to devote more time to assessing the work of individual children and thus help them progress. Progress is also likely as a result of the gradual improvement of quality of entry to the teaching profession on account of increasing graduate qualification and more rigorous selection procedures. Increasingly, too, in-service training courses are being devoted to assessment and record-keeping. The Department's own course on the subject now runs twice a year, and is always fully subscribed. Most other DES courses pay attention to these aspects.

There is a need for teachers to become familiar with the whole range of work of which pupils are capable, from the occasional really outstanding piece of writing or creative mathematics by a gifted child to the efforts of a less able child which reveal all kinds of difficulties of spelling, writing and structure. Teachers need to be able to spot the clues with which work of this kind often bristles, for one of the most important things to realise is that not until we give children opportunities to talk, to write, actually to *do* something, can they show us where their strengths and difficulties lie. For example, a child may have a problem with reversals or perhaps another has a total misunderstanding of notation in mathematics, but such difficulties only emerge in the course of their work. Then they enable teachers to begin to pinpoint the difficulty and look for more sensitive diagnostic tests and suitable material to grapple with it effectively. Thoughtful observation of this kind has led many teachers to devise their own diagnostic assessments.

Language Assessment

Much assessment has to do with skills of numeracy and literacy. The Bullock Report (1975) argued for more careful assessment and more systematic monitoring of language skills. Though teachers have always taken language skills seriously, that report did help to focus attention upon many important and specific aspects of language development which merited closer attention. In the NFER survey of reading which took place concurrently with the primary survey, an average score of 31·13 out of a possible 60 was achieved by 4955 11 year olds. This is consistent with a rising trend in reading standards between 1955 (when the score was 28·71) and 1976–77. However, there is reason to believe that higher order reading skills involving, for example, inference, comparison, close reading and skimming are not always taught and are seldom consciously assessed.

On this theme the survey adds:

'The teaching of reading is regarded by teachers as extremely important, and the basic work in this skill is undertaken systematically. The levels of ability of the children inevitably vary, but those who find learning to read difficult are more likely to be given work suitably matched to their abilities than the children who are more able readers.'

Too often, the teaching of reading emphasises decoding skills. Children read in groups to one another and to the teacher, but the transition to silent reading or to the varied uses of reading is left to take care of itself. Once the reading series is complete children tend to get on to free readers or library choice and what they do with such freedom is sometimes anyone's guess. And yet the demands made on children by work in other subjects such as history, geography, science and mathematics at the late primary and secondary stages are often varied and specific. Reading for factual information is probably the simplest but reading for inference—'what does the writer feel or think about this issue?' is more subtle. Also reading for methodological information—how to bake a cake or assemble a kit or understand how a radio works—can involve highly focused reading. Children need the experience of having to read a sentence or a line of poetry several times or in several different ways to wrest its full meaning or savour its whole essence. Skimming, too—so important for the efficient library researcher (or even browser) and vital for anyone whose sanity depends on spotting the things that need *not* be read—is a skill which needs to be taught and should be assessed at school.

Tests of these and other skills have been developed for the APU language surveys and should be available via the NFER's LEA's and Schools' Item Bank Project (LEASIB) before long. Meanwhile, such tests are not too difficult for the individual teacher to devise herself.

Writing has always featured prominently in most areas of the curriculum but the various forms of writing have received different kinds of treatment. The science teacher may look for clear explanation, the historian for sound argument, the geographer for accurate content; all or none may correct spelling, punctuation or faulty syntax. The English teacher may set formal exercises designed to teach punctuation, précis and paragraphing, irrespective of content. Purely transactional writing is usually and regularly marked against specific criteria, but expressive pieces of writing in prose or poetry are sometimes assessed only holistically or impressionistically. As a teacher once said to me, 'I don't correct spelling mistakes in the project work; it spoils the books. We deal with that kind of thing by exercises and spelling tests.' Such ambivalence, whatever other advantages it has, does not best serve the teaching of language across the curriculum; though undeniably, a holistic element is as essential to the assessment of sizeable pieces of written work as it is to the judgment of artifacts in craft or music.

Spoken language and listening comprehension, by contrast, are hardly ever assessed, though we all employ these language skills far more frequently than those of reading and writing. In the Schools Council project on record-keeping in primary schools only about 33 per cent of the schools made any record of spoken language development and not all of these were based upon systematic assessment. Very occasionally a primary school will make a special point of encouraging excellence in drama and spoken English but usually oral mother tongue language is not specifically assessed. Teachers may claim 'of course we care . . . but we haven't got time'. If this is the case—how can they be sure that pupils are progressing?

Assessing Mathematical Skills

On mathematics, the primary survey has various points to make. Here too, 4991 of the 11 year olds took a 50 item NFER test. The item facilities were such that a mean score of about 25 was anticipated; in the event, the average turned out to be 27·97. The primary school sample differed from that for which the original facility values had been calculated and so the means were not strictly comparable.

However, there is evidence from many different quarters that pupils find difficulty with questions aimed at the principles underlying the basic skills and with questions involving how and when to *apply* them. So often all that is required is the successful operation of a rule irrespective of the rationale of the method or generality of the result. Some good examples of this occurred among the responses to the 50 item test. For instance, questions involving reading a result straight off a simple bar chart, giving correct change out of a pound note, spotting tangram pieces which make a square, and identifying simple geometrical nets were all well answered. But the question $16 \times 35 = 560$, so $17 \times 35 = 560+?$ caused much difficulty. Many children carried out the multiplication 17×35 and subtracted, not always arriving at the correct answer. Relatively few saw that 17×35 is 1×35 *more* than 16×35 and must therefore be $560 + 35$. Similar failures to

35

grasp underlying principles resulted from another question which gave a set of statements about a hidden three-digit number and asked which were bound to be true. A question which asked pupils to ring the smallest fraction out of $\frac{1}{2}$, $\frac{3}{4}$, $\frac{3}{8}$, $\frac{1}{4}$ and $\frac{5}{8}$ was answered correctly by only 40 per cent of the pupils. Most surprising of all [as Norman Thomas points out in Chapter 1], a question giving a simple graph for converting miles to kilometres and requiring pupils to convert 1·6 kilometres to miles attracted only 28 per cent of correct responses.

Clearly there are lessons to be learnt here. Likewise, in the findings of the first APU mathematics survey there is a wealth of data which should help to indicate areas of strength and other areas in the subject requiring attention.

Sometimes successful mathematics teaching requires the *diagnosis* of particular difficulties. Some youngster cannot get the hang of notation—where to place the decimal point. A younger child may mistake 23 and 32. Another gets into a pickle over carrying figures or setting out a multiplication or a division sum. Often it is possible to pinpoint the precise nature of the difficulty by the selection and use of a carefully devised diagnostic test.

A good deal of assessment in classroom mathematics is simply concerned with *mastery learning*. Has Jimmy Smith—or the whole class—progressed enough and acquired sufficient mastery in this topic to go on to the next one? Certainly that is a question which must often be asked—and answered.

Science

When it comes to the teaching of science in primary schools, the survey makes discouraging reading.

'Few primary schools visited in the course of this survey had effective programmes for the teaching of science. There was a lack of appropriate equipment; insufficient attention was given to ensuring proper coverage of key scientific notions;

the teaching of processes and skills such as observing, the formulation of hypotheses, experimenting and recording was often superficial. The work in observational and experimental science was less well matched to childrens' capabilities than work in any other area of the curriculum.'

It is of course fairly straightforward to check on remembered facts but much less easy to discover whether children are thinking scientifically. Since there is no question of laying down a syllabus or prescribing facts to be remembered, the APU science assessments are mainly about processes, such as observation, collecting, tabulating, recording and illustrating data; looking for trends in it and suggesting possible explanations. This in turn involves the design and execution of experiments to decide the order of probability of the hypotheses or explanations. The APU science monitoring teams have devised written and practical assessments of each of these activities. Some of them will be conducted with individual children, others with groups of children. The instruments themselves should produce helpful ideas for teachers for use in their own classrooms. Examples of items already piloted may be seen in the APU Science Progress Report 1977/78, which is based on consultations with teachers of science all over the country.

Other Areas of the Curriculum

What has been said so far applies equally to history and geography. For while these subjects may have distinctive ways of looking at the world and of deducing conclusions from evidence, they nevertheless rely heavily upon the range of language, mathematical and empirical thinking skills already discussed.

But in the expressive arts where statements are made through quite different media such as sound, movement, paint, clay, fabric or even food, using quite different symbol systems such as musical notation, choreographic notation, line, texture, form etc., the problems of assessment are very different. Indeed the *purposes* of expression in these curriculum areas may differ from those in the more prosaic activities. A creation such as a dance, or a painting or a piece of music may aim to describe a location such as Fingal's Cave or an event such as the 1812 Overture. But it may have less literal or specific aims and seek to create a mood or feeling of exultation or sorrow. It may be designed to make a statement as Picasso's 'Guernica' did—or as a dance or ballet may. It may simply evince sensual delight by its very existence. Indeed, music and the arts would probably not exist if it were possible to say better in words or figures or diagrams, the kind of things that they do proclaim.

Assessment in these areas is very different but every bit as necessary to progress and high performance as in the three Rs. It is simply not good enough to provide paint and sound sources and leave the results to the expressive initiative of pupils. In each of the visual, aural or kinesthetic arts there are at least four distinctly assessable areas—a body of useful basic knowledge, a variety of receptive and perceptive skills, a core of creative techniques, and an analytical, appreciative capacity. For example, aesthetic expression through music may be enhanced by a factual knowledge of notation, pitch, and scales—of the sounds and ranges of instruments—of principles of harmony and simple counterpoint. Making and appreciating it requires a trained ear, an ability to listen or follow a theme, certain reading skills and maybe the ability to actually perform upon an instrument. Appreciation probably depends upon being able to synthesise experiences of the previous three. Clearly, knowledge and perception can be and have been tested for a long time: there is no shortage of means or experience. Performance skills, particularly in music, have been assessed not only in schools but by the Royal School of Music examinations and in all manner of festivals and competitions. Generally speaking such assessment has been carried out by specialist teachers and it is worth recalling the comments of the primary survey about the commendable degree of match achieved by specialist teachers.

Admittedly, there are products of the expressive arts which are difficult to assess. Subjective or holistic judgments about an abstract—or for that matter a non-abstract piece of sculpture—may vary; one man's meat is another man's poison. But assessment is not really about liking or exercising personal fads but about applying agreed, reasonable criteria. Even in these difficult areas a great deal of modern research suggests that it is possible to develop reliable measures of scoring based upon such criteria.

Problems Associated with Organisation

Given carefully devised assessments in the various areas of the primary curriculum their ease of administration is often affected by organisation. As the HMIs note in para 8.34 of the primary survey, in a large class of children with a wide range of abilities the sheer physical problem of making regular assessments of children all doing different pieces of work can present formidable difficulties. It may indeed be the case that this problem is tied up with the other major concern of the survey—the under-achievement of the ablest pupils in any given class. For it is not difficult to understand that a teacher may feel obliged to spend time in helping slower children and leave the ablest to their own devices. Even if the work set for the ablest is carefully planned and on the whole appropriate, there may not remain sufficient time to devote to its careful assessment when there is so much to correct and rectify in the efforts of the less able children.

Micro-technology, particularly micro-electronics, carries rich promise for a good deal of labour saving in the routine aspects of assessment and recording. There are many schools in North America where all the attendance records are computerised, and where much of the day to day class assessment is machine markable and where the results are scored and stored by computer. Of course, such advances carry dangers against which we will have to be vigilant. But they can also undoubtedly be harnessed wisely to help teachers overcome some of the more menial tasks involved in assessment.

Key Issues needing Resolution

In the earlier sections I have tried to indicate some of the benefits of assessment and the need to consider new approaches in areas such as speaking and listening, expressive work in art, music, dance and poetry, and maybe even in some broader aspects of personal and social development. But these are matters for heads and teachers to debate and decide in their own schools.

A second key issue is that of sifting, digesting and using effectively the information we are now obtaining. During the last year or so many educational concerns have involved assessment of one kind or another. These were summarised in Report on Education No. 93 and included also screening for handicap as discussed in the Warnock Report and that set of issues involved with common examinations at 16+ as discussed in the Waddell Report. 1980 has seen the publication of the results of the first APU primary mathematics survey of 11 year olds carried out in May 1978. Two further mathematics surveys and the first two language surveys of 11 and 16 year olds will take place, and the results made public in 1980 or early 1981. In 1980 seven surveys are planned—two in mathematics, two in language and three in science at ages 11, 13 and 16. By 1981 the mathematics reports may begin to show trends. They may even begin to indicate whether any action resulting from the earlier mathematics reports is starting to produce desirable results.

Somehow or other all this information has to be disseminated and assimilated. It will need to be discussed by inspectors and advisers, by teacher associations of all kinds and by groups of teachers working together in teachers' centres. It is greatly to be hoped that it produces beneficial action. The last thing we need is a mountain of assessment information whose existence makes no difference whatsoever to the system we are all working to improve.

In conclusion, it is important to stress that in making the above quotations and comments a deliberate attempt has been made to highlight points which relate to assessment. There is much to commend in the work of teachers and pupils; the high priorities that are given to the teaching of basic skills, the importance attached to children acquiring a sense of social responsibility and the quiet working atmosphere which is established in the great majority of classes when needed. But this chapter is about assessment and assessment is about helping children to progress and improve their performance.

4
Continuity
Joan Dean

On transfer from infant to junior school Jackie was reading at an average level for her age although she was below average in intelligence. She was beginning to write quite well after a slow start in spite of inadequate phonic knowledge. In number she had problems in spite of much effort by her teachers. In the junior school she went to the class of a teacher who had previously taught 11 year olds. Though a good teacher in many ways, he found difficulty in adjusting to this change. In particular he had had very little experience of teaching children who had not yet established basic skills. The records which came with the children gave general opinions rather than specific information about what the children did and did not know, and since the head believed in delegating and letting people find their own feet, it was well on in the year before Jackie's problems were even appreciated and the work generally did not meet her needs.

Jason's third year in an 8–12 middle school was spent with a teacher who believed in making children independent learners. Children were trained to plan and organise work for themselves within a clear structure and to use resources. They learned to use longer and longer periods of time to work together in groups and in the process they achieved high standards in many aspects of their work, particularly when it involved creative and inventive thinking. They also became very independent. Jason thrived on this programme and did extremely well. He then moved to the fourth-year class which was taken by a teacher with an entirely different view which the head felt might be a useful preparation for the secondary school. Desks were in rows and there was a strict timetable. Children were expected to conform. They were given little opportunity to show their ability to plan and organise their own work and to demonstrate their skill in reasoning and creativity. They were encouraged to be competitive rather than cooperative and independence was firmly discouraged. Jason found life was more difficult than formerly and was in trouble for doing what his previous teacher had encouraged.

Gerald was a child with serious learning problems. He attended a good middle school but his parents saw his failure as a failure on the part of the school and were critical of the methods of teaching and learning employed there. When he reached the age of transfer to secondary school his parents decided against the secondary school to which children from this particular middle school normally went, choosing to send him to a prestigious school on the other side of the town which had been reorganised from a grammar school two years earlier and was noted for its traditional approaches and academic success with able children. Gerald's middle school had built up very good relationships with its neighbouring secondary school, but not with the school his parents had chosen. Nevertheless, records were sent on, giving details of his problems and what had been tried. Gerald himself was enthusiastic about going to his new school and set out happily on the first day in his new school uniform. Unfortunately, the teachers in his new school took the view that they liked to make their own judgments without looking at the views of their primary school colleagues. Many of them were also unused to dealing with children with serious learning problems. Gerald was therefore absorbed into a very specialist timetable and given teaching which made demands that he was quite unable to meet. Since his difficulties were not generally appreciated he also found himself having to reveal his inadequacies publicly at an early stage when a teacher asked him to read aloud.

43

Discontinuities

These three children all experienced discontinuity which could well have serious consequences for their development and learning. None of the schools concerned was a bad school and none of the teachers was a poor teacher; in the classes of all three children there were others who flourished. Yet these were not isolated cases in the three schools. Nor are similar cases unusual in other schools. There are many occasions when teachers learn to deal with new situations at the expense of the children they teach. There are situations when teachers are critical of what has happened previously and miss the strengths of the past experience. There are teachers who do not build on what has gone before; teachers who start their pupils all over again from the beginning without noting what has been done; teachers who mistrust their professional colleagues and are not interested in what they say, and so on.

There are also discontinuities in the treatment of children. Anyone looking at 7 year olds in an infant school or 8 year olds in a first school in July, will be conscious of their independence and confidence as the oldest children in the school. This is even more the case at the top of the junior or middle school. Much is often expected of them and many live up to these expectations. In September they are the 'little' ones again and very often expectations are far lower. It is, for example, salutary to note the extent to which primary school children are expected to work unsupervised and the rarity of this expectation in the secondary school below the level of the sixth form.

There is also discontinuity in the way the curriculum and the learning programme are built up. A recent study in my own authority of the way time was spent in a group of 8–12 middle schools and the secondary school to which the children went showed that 20 per cent of time in the middle school was spent on some form of individual project-type study, varying in quality, but usually involving some of the skills of independent learning. This disappeared completely in the secondary school, where all the time was allocated to specific subject learning.

Discontinuity may also be fostered by the organisation within the LEA. Staffing and resource provision for primary and secondary schools may not be viewed as a continuum but may be decided separately using different criteria, sometimes by separate committees. LEA administrators and advisers may also have separated responsibilities and while this does not necessarily lead to a lack of continuity, it can do so.

This is not to suggest that different stages of education should operate in the same way. Change can stimulate and it is part of a child's growing up. It becomes a matter for concern when the change is so great that it interferes with the child's learning, as it did with Jason, or when the lack of information about a child, or unwillingness or inability to use it leads to unsuitable and possibly counter-productive teaching, as it did with Gerald and Jackie. Education is a continuous process in the experience of each child [as Norman Thomas stresses on page 14] and we need to make the curve of continuity a smooth one from teacher to teacher, class to class and school to school.

Issues of continuity have received relatively limited attention in the recent primary survey by HMI. Consideration of continuity was not included in the schedule of observation (in itself, somewhat surprising) and does not appear in the conclusions. It was therefore, presumably, a matter for only incidental observation. There were some interesting findings, however, which suggest that while there is a reasonable amount of attention given to continuity within the school, the emphasis at transition tends to be on easing the problems for the child with 'the importance of continuity in the curriculum of the schools . . . largely overlooked'. This would seem to be an important finding which gives cause for concern. It is therefore somewhat surprising that it merits only one paragraph in the text and no comment elsewhere.

Goals

The idea of continuity implies the existence of goals towards which teaching and learning are directed and of planning which gradually leads children to their attainment. These need discussion at every level and most of all within individual schools and groups of schools, not with the idea that everyone should do the same things, but that there should be enough common ground to make each child's learning a continuous process.

There is firstly a matter of identifying goals which can be broadly agreed. These need to be concerned with understanding and skills in different aspects of the curriculum, perhaps more than with its content, although the content is the raw material from which understanding, skill and the ability to use knowledge can be developed. The primary survey suggests that we have a great deal of work to do in clarifying our thinking and establishing a sense of direction in subjects such as science and environmental studies even within schools, let alone between stages of education. If goals are seen in fairly broad terms there is no reason why they should be limiting. It might, for example, be possible to agree that all junior or middle schools contributing to a particular secondary school or schools should undertake a local study which involved field work, included some historical, geographical, sociological and scientific work and attempted to develop some agreed skills and concepts. A group of schools working together at this could develop a variety of approaches and materials from which teachers could select, and these would be common ground on which the secondary school could build without too much limitation for anyone. The advantage of this kind of approach is that it gives an opportunity to set different goals for different children while providing some common ground for everyone. It is perhaps worth remembering that within the schools of an LEA there will probably be a few children at the end of the primary stage who could manage O-level in some subjects and others who still have serious difficulties in reading and basic number.

A child's development and learning are more than the acquisition of skill, knowledge and understanding, however. As Mike Hill stresses in Chapter 11, we live in a fast-changing society and this has important implications for education; implications which we have only partly understood and accepted at present. Knowledge itself is changing and there is no longer any way that schooling can equip a child with knowledge for all that lies ahead. What we know is that he will need to change, adapt and learn afresh and this means that his ability to meet new situations and challenges is important. He needs confidence to meet the unknown, strategies to tackle new problems and the ability to deal with new knowledge. All of this suggests that the process of this learning at school and the way he structures what he knows are very important. Much of this learning takes place as a by-product of acquiring content. Perhaps it needs to be more clearly in our minds than formerly. Certainly we need to assess progress towards goals of this kind and deliberately build into what we do the development of the skills which enable a child to become an independent learner.

There is also a need to look at personal and social development as a continuous process. We need to work together to find ways of helping children to develop desirable qualities for learning such as curiosity, persistence and inventiveness. We also need to foster other qualities, such as understanding of others, capacity for taking responsibility, ability to form and maintain relationships, as well as providing social skills such as the ability to express needs and views, to question and enquire, to work with others to agreed ends and to cope with a wide variety of social situations. Individual teachers very often help children to develop in these ways, but a school-wide policy and approach are needed.

Demands for particular kinds of behaviour also create discontinuity. It can be salutary to follow a particular child for a day in a large secondary school to see the variety of demands made upon him and the ways in which he needs to adjust to different teachers. This is less of a problem at the primary stage, but we could often help children more over this kind of adjustment if we talked about it with them and looked at what is involved in assessing each situation for the child. It is the child with the most difficulty in learning who is often most confused over adjusting to different adults. Security to some extent depends upon knowing one's boundaries. Children begin to feel secure with a teacher when they know what is required of them, what is and is not allowed and the teacher's likely reactions. While a measure of insecurity can be stimulating, too much can be counter-productive and a child may spend time working out what the teacher wants and guessing the right answers, rather than concentrating on the material under consideration.

Policies

If we accept that there is a need for a longer term view of education and greater emphasis on continuity than we have at present, we need to consider how it can be achieved. There is first of all a need for commitment to the idea of continuity from everyone involved in education: the survey could perhaps have given a stronger lead here.

No progress can be made in improving continuity unless individual teachers and schools are convinced that this is necessary. Improved continuity may mean the sacrifice of some autonomy, working with other teachers and agreeing to do certain things in certain ways. It means that each teacher must try to see where his work fits into the overall pattern for each child. It means keeping records for the benefit of others and using the records others have written. This is all time-consuming, often difficult and it requires a professional appreciation of the need for continuity.

The most important factor for continuity within the school is probably the extent to which teachers work together and think about long-term planning. Children are in an infant school for two or three years, in a first school for three, four or five and a junior or middle school for four years. However, it is rare for the school to plan so far ahead as this, looking at the way in which teacher knowledge and skill can be built up and planning developments sufficiently far ahead to build up resources. It is true that it is not possible to predict levels of staffing or capitation so far ahead, but this makes long-term planning even more important. If a key member of staff leaves, it is doubly important to see that others are developing skills which would enable them to take over. If resources may be increasingly difficult to acquire, then their purchase needs to be planned over a considerable period. Every school staff needs to discuss continuity and long-term planning. Teachers are more likely to feel commitment to common plans where they have been involved in decision- and policy-making about curriculum and resources. Such discussions foster teacher development and help ensure a more continuous education for each child.

The use of a written scheme of work links with this. The scheme in each area of the curriculum may be drawn up by the head or by someone with a coordinating rôle, but unless the teachers using it really make it their own, it may serve little purpose. It needs either to be drawn up through staff discussion and then regularly reviewed or it needs to be the subject of a series of discussions.

Discussion also needs to go on among 'families' of feeder and receiver schools if curriculum continuity advocated in the primary survey is not to be overlooked. There should be inter-visiting, exchange of ideas and information and a following through of individual children. Copies of schemes and syllabuses need to be exchanged and discussed as well as records. It can also be valuable to exchange teachers for a time so that each school comes to understand the other.

Record-keeping is an essential ingredient in making education continuous. We need to give thought to how we can provide records for each child which give teaching information which is easily accessible and useful, rather than expressions of opinion about potential. If one teacher is to be able to take on from where the last teacher left off with an individual child or a group of children, what he needs to know is what the child or group have or have not done, know or do not know. He needs to know what has been tried and with what success and where there have been problems and difficulties. If a school is wanting to group children on entry, then information about reading ages and potential is useful, but it is of limited value in helping a teacher to decide what to teach and how to teach it.

It is in the early years of schooling that teachers perhaps come nearest to recording this kind of information, but as the child grows older, it becomes more difficult to identify what he does and does not know and the practice tends to change to one of recording grades and adding brief comments. It is even rare to find a record of the courses and books used, yet this could very often be duplicated for a group of children and individual variation recorded. Our record systems at the later stages of education seem more concerned with sorting and grouping children than with seeing that each is getting a continuous education matched to his needs. This is not to deny the need to grade for some purposes, but to suggest that what many schools do at present is of limited value because insufficent thought has been given to the child's long-term needs and the kind of information which is useful for a whole range of purposes. Grading, for example, would be of more value if it were used to identify areas of concern within a subject. It is of limited teaching value to know that, overall, Gillian has a C for English, but if the record indicates that Gillian's ability to write in creative and personal ways is graded A, her ability in spelling is E, and she tends to be only average ability in more factual writing, the receiving teacher has useful information to work on, especially if the meaning of the grading system has been carefully considered and agreed.

A great deal of valuable staff development can be fostered

within a school if the staff work together to try to provide a check-list of progress in different areas of curriculum. This can then be used, in part at least, as a record for each child. This has the advantage that teachers have thought it through together and thus have a commitment to it. It also ensures that at least part of the content of the scheme of work is familiar to everyone. A further development is to work at this within a 'family' of schools so that the group of schools has an agreed long-term record in various aspects of work.

Continuity is what is or is not experienced by the individual child. He is the one who experiences the discontinuity of demands by different teachers and different schools. His parents may also have an awareness of what is happening to him which is different from that of his teachers. We can learn a good deal from talking with children and their parents about what has happened to them. It can also help if we encourage both children and their parents to see and plan ahead and make a point of explaining our goals to them more frequently than we sometimes do. There are many occasions when, by not making our goals explicit, a school or a teacher loses the advantage of harnessing the child's desire to learn and the parent's desire to support him.

But it is not only the teachers and the schools who need to be committed and concerned with continuity. The LEA needs to have a commitment to long-term planning and continuity and the extent of this commitment will be reflected in the way it attempts to provide resources, particularly teachers, to see children through what has been started, perhaps by building a time-lapse into calculations for staffing and capitation at a time of falling rolls. This is further helped if there is a measure of virement in the use of resources. It should perhaps be noted in passing that it is difficult for an LEA to reconcile continuity and parental choice: both seem to be highly desirable but are conflicting.

We also need this commitment nationally. Local and national policies tend to work against continuity when the major parties hold radically different views. The 'Great Debate' and the Green Paper which followed, together with various reports, and in particular, the primary survey, have provided schools with much food for thought which needs to be assimilated and interpreted to meet the needs of individual children. Schools, therefore, need some honest assurance in a time of diminishing numbers that resources will be available so that they can plan ahead. It may well be better to face and accept a not very generous provision which can be maintained, than to be buoyed up with promises which prove impossible to fulfil.

We have given lip service to the idea of continuity for many years. Continuity will only happen when our commitment is sufficient to give it a high level of priority. There is a very real need to do so.

5

Matching

Wynne Harlen

Survey Findings

The Plowden Report contained many thought-provoking passages, but one stands out as capturing most succinctly what is of import and challenge to all concerned with children's learning:

'Learning is a continuous process from birth. The teacher's task is to provide an environment and opportunities which are sufficiently challenging for children and yet not so difficult as to be outside their reach. There has to be the right mixture of the familiar and the novel, the right match to the stage of learning the child has reached. If the material is too familiar or the learning skills too easy, children will become inattentive and bored. If too great maturity is demanded of them, they fall back on half remembered formulae and become concerned only to give the reply the teacher wants. Children can think and form concepts, so long as they work at their own level, and are not made to feel that they are failures.'

Para. 533 (CACE 1967)

The concept of 'match' was taken as one important theme in the HMI survey of primary schools, where an attempt was made to quantify the 'degree of match' for children in different ability groups within their class in various subject areas. These

53

Data on success in matching (HMI Survey report pp. 86–87)

Table 1 Classes achieving reasonably satisfactory match for less able groups

	Less able groups		
Percentage of classes	7 year old classes	9 year old classes	11 year old classes
94–85	Reading	Reading	Reading
84–75	Mathematics Writing Spoken language Physical education	Mathematics Writing	Mathematics Writing
74–65	Music	Spoken language Physical education Music	Spoken language Physical education History
64–55	Art and craft	History	Music Geography
54–45	History Geography	Geography	Art and craft
44–35	Science (observational) Science (experimental)	Art and craft Science (observational)	Science (observational) Science (experimental)
34–25	–	Science (experimental)	–

data provide, at last, some measure (however crude) of how well matching is carried out in schools. For some areas of the curriculum, notably science and the humanities, the findings are not happy ones. But they are not surprising to anyone who is closely involved in primary education, and they cannot be easily dismissed. Arguments have been advanced that matching is not important, indeed that learning can take place better when there is 'mismatching' (Neville Bennett, *TES*, 3 Nov. 1978), but I believe such arguments suggest a difference of interpretation of matching rather than a serious disclaimer of matching as proposed here. It is clearly important to discuss just what we do mean by matching and the part it plays in helping learning. Firstly, however, we take a more detailed look at the findings in the HMI survey about matching.

To appreciate the full weight of the survey results about matching it is necessary to look at all the three tables for less

Table 2 Classes achieving reasonably satisfactory match for the average groups

	Average groups		
Percentage of classes	7 year old classes	9 year old classes	11 year old classes
94–85	Reading	Reading	–
84–75	Mathematics	Mathematics	Reading Mathematics
74–65	Physical education Writing Spoken language Music	Physical education Writing	Physical education Writing Spoken language
64–55	–	Spoken language Music	Music History
54–45	History Art and craft	History	Geography
44–35	Geography Science (observational)	Geography Art and craft	Art and craft Science (observational)
34–25	Science (experimental)	Science (observational)	Science (experimental)
24–20	–	Science (experimental)	–

Table 3 Classes achieving reasonably satisfactory match for more able groups

	More able groups		
Percentage of classes	7 year old classes	9 year old classes	11 year old classes
64–55	Reading Physical education Spoken language	Reading Physical education	Reading Physical education
54–45	Mathematics Music Writing	Mathematics Music	Mathematics Music Spoken language
44–35	Art and craft	Writing Spoken language	Writing
34–25	History Geography	–	Art and craft History
24–15	Science (observational) Science (experimental)	Art and craft History Geography Science (observational)	Geography Science (observational) Science (experimental)
14–10	–	Science (experimental)	–

55

able, average and more able groups, each at three age levels (Tables 1–3). The judgment as to ability level was made by the teachers and this part of the method of gathering the data has been criticised. These criticisms do not, however, weaken the force of these results, for what happens in a classroom that affects matching depends on the teacher's views of the ability of individual pupils, not on a more objective measure of ability not known to the teacher. The striking patterns in these results hardly need to be pointed out. It is clear that the order of success in matching among different subjects varies little, with reading, mathematics, writing and physical education being consistently near the top of the scale. At the bottom, with heavy constancy, is science, with geography and history, art and craft not far ahead. It is also clear that the proportion of good match improves from the more able to the average to the less able and, to a smaller extent, from older to younger pupils.

Interpretations

How can we interpret these findings? As a concerned science educationist I might put the question more pointedly: why is science always at the bottom of the pile, not only in matching, but also, as is clear elsewhere in the report (Chapter 5 iv) in the provision of adequate time and equipment? There is something more important at stake here, though, than just the interest of one subject area and the question has to be discussed in more general terms. The survey itself confirmed what many teachers would like to believe, that 'the range of work and the standards achieved are related, sometimes in ways that are not immediately obvious; for example, a narrow concentration on teaching a skill is not always the best way of achieving high standards in it' (6.1). The inclusion of a range of subjects beyond the 'basics' is thus seen to be not only worthwhile for development in these subjects but also for the 'basics' themselves. However, it is in the subjects 'beyond the basics', the art, the humanities, the sciences, that 'matching' is least

56

apparent. Thus we return to the question of how this comes about.

There are several possible factors which might well be associated, though no one could be described as *the* cause. Firstly, the order of descending success in matching is also the order of descending 'importance' of subjects, as seen in most people's eyes. This is a fact which is largely common knowledge, but also has the support of research. The project on 'The Aims of Primary Education' reported that the results of teachers' ratings of different aims were that 'conspicuous by their complete absence among the priority aims were any references to the arts, music, physical education, religious education, sex education, science or a second language. Aims in all of these areas were congregated in the lower half of the rank order and most of them failed to reach even an average rank of "important".' (Ashton *et al.*, 1975 p. 62). We may regret that the notion of what is basic, and therefore important, in primary education does not extend to the concepts which help children understand the physical, human and social world around them, but it cannot be denied that this is the case at present. Also, it will take a great deal of time for any change in the established priorities. Putting this together with the 'matching' findings might suggest that what teachers do not consider important they do not teach very well. But it is too early to draw such conclusions, for there are other factors to be considered.

The second factor which may be associated with success in matching is a reflection of what is important in initial training programmes. Teachers cannot be expected to teach subjects well if their preparation in these subjects has been insufficient. Again it does not need any suspension of credibility to accept that the order of success in matching correlates with the order of time spent in training in the various subject areas. The peculiar difference which exists in some cases between what teachers are expected to do when in service and what their training covers is hard to understand. For example, the pri-

57

mary survey, whilst endorsing the use of posts of responsibility to provide a teacher with knowledge and ability to give leadership in planning and guiding work, did not advocate specialist teaching. In schools, each teacher is expected, with some help, to be able to deal with science, history, geography, and so on, yet there is a significant proportion of teachers leaving initial training courses without any training in teaching science and in at least one of the humanities.

A third factor might well be teachers' own background knowledge. In science this must certainly be very significant and could be no less important for history, geography, art and craft. At the primary level it is not important for pupils to learn about particular periods in history, particular facts in science, and so on, but rather to begin to develop concepts and study skills which can be applied to a range of subject matter. However, to do this it is necessary for there to be *some* content to study [as Robert Dearden points out in Chapter 2]; one does not learn to observe without observing *something*, or to reason logically without reasoning about *something*, or about how living things behave without studying some particular living things. A lack of knowledge of relevant facts, even though these do not have to be transmitted to the children, is undoubtedly inhibiting to a teacher. In science, particularly, we then have a situation leading to a vicious circle—of pupils having no adequate science experiences in the primary school, being deterred by academic science courses in the secondary school and leaving with a dislike of the subject, some to become teachers who perpetuate these conditions.

A fourth factor relates to the kind of materials which teachers have to help them. At the top end of the matching ratings we find reading and mathematics, for which ready worked out teaching schemes and materials abound. If he or she so wishes a teacher can use sets of books, for pupils and teacher, and associated aids which, on account of their structure, ensure a fair basis for matching. Such materials can never replace the sensitive interaction of teachers with pupils which is necessary for matching, but they at least provide the essential resources. As we go down the matching scale the degree of structure in materials recently produced for teachers declines. This is inevitable since, as already mentioned, these are subjects where complex concepts and sophisticated study skills are the aim, rather than mastery of a well-defined set of facts and procedures. Structure of the same kind as in reading schemes is thus not appropriate, but structure of a different kind *is* appropriate. It could be such as to indicate the development of various concepts in children and exemplify subject matter which would foster it. Instead of this, much material for teachers tends to suggest isolated activities or topics which are not obviously related to the systematic development of underlying concepts and skills.

There may well be other factors which could be postulated as correlating with success in matching; it is likely to be a combination of factors, those mentioned and others, which accounts for differential success in matching. We can come a little nearer to finding the most likely causes by looking now at what is the meaning of matching, what it entails and why it is important. Support for its importance comes not only from the opinions of experienced educationists, as represented in the paragraph quoted above from the Plowden Report, but also from the findings of those who have studied children's mental development, for example Bruner (1960) and Piaget (1970), who may disagree on other matters but are of one voice in regard to matching. From a different angle again Bloom (1971) has pointed out the damaging consequences of mismatching.

The Meaning of Matching

Perhaps the first point to make about matching is that it does *not* mean giving children more of what they can already do. It is this misuse of the term which I believe is responsible for claims that learning is better when there is mismatching. What matching does mean, in simple terms, is finding out what children can already do and what ideas they have, as a basis for providing experiences which will develop these skills and concepts. The keynote of matching is thus finding the right challenge for a child, the size of step that he can take by using but also extending existing ideas. There is as much a mismatch if this step is too small, leading to boredom, as there is if it is too large, leading to failure.

The second point is to recognise that while this may seem reasonable and indeed obvious in theory, it is extremely difficult to translate into practice. The process of learning is dynamic, not static, and 'what children can do' is changing constantly. Furthermore, even if the difficulty of matching could be overcome for one child, the teacher has the problem of attempting this for thirty or more individuals, all varying in past experience, background and existing ideas. A child who can work at a more advanced level will be underoccupied by activities which provide a worthwhile challenge for another. The teacher has thus not only to attempt to cater for a multitude of differences between pupils but also to distinguish easy success, accompanied by signs of boredom and lack of interest, from success which results from a challenge which has made a pupil try hard and has resulted in some development in his thinking.

As if these complexities were not enough, we have further to acknowledge that it is not just the intellectual demand of an activity which has to be matched to the level from which the pupils can operate, but that there are other features of learners and learning experiences which have to be matched as well as possible. Past experiences and knowledge gained out of school interact with school activities, so that children will react differently to them. We find an obvious example of this in children's reactions to swimming classes at school; generally, reactions range from over-enthusiasm to cowering resistance. These reactions are physical and thus clearly observable, but there must be the same range of less observable reactions to the sight of the maths book or the sound of the word 'project'.

In addition there are, of course, individual differences in interests, attitudes, preferred modes of learning and time required for particular activities.

All this might seem to suggest that hope has to be abandoned of putting into practice the idea of matching. But what it points to is that a solution in terms of a prescription or a set of guidelines cannot be expected. There is, however, a strategy which can be adopted for improving the degree of matching, whilst it has to be admitted that the theoretical ideal of complete matching for every pupil all the time is unattainable. In teaching, decisions are all the time being made, to adapt or adjust materials, methods, organisation, pupil–pupil and pupil–teacher interactions. The aim of these decisions is to help the children's learning and it is through examining how these decisions are made that we can see how matching can be improved.

Fig. 1 (after Harlen, 1978) looks at the decisions the teacher makes and the influences on such decision-making.

Here the teacher, subject to external constraints and other influences, including his or her own ability, which limit the

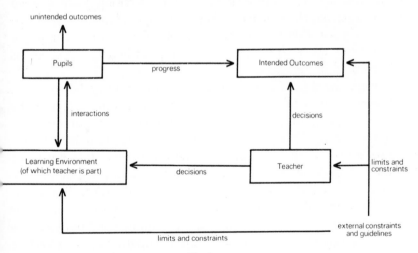

Fig.1

range of options, makes decisions about the learning environment and the intended outcomes. The phrase 'learning environment' is used here to convey the whole set of conditions arising from decisions about materials, methods, the teacher's rôle, etc., which affect the pupils' learning. The interaction of pupils and learning environment changes them both; the changes in the pupils may be both intended and unintended. There would be nothing wrong with this scheme of decision-making if we knew exactly how to bring about intended learning. But this is not the case, for, as already mentioned, there are many factors influencing learning which make each situation unique. To take them into account the teacher needs more information as a basis for decisions than is suggested in the diagram. Since there are no prescriptions to be found for matching to every different set of circumstances, it is necessary to do this by a series of adjustments made in response to information about what is happening. Information is needed about pupils' ideas and about interactions of pupils with the learning environment so that the moment-to-moment decisions can respond to what is taking place. Instead of suggesting the teacher makes decisions independently of the response of the pupils, the model of decision-making for matching must show feedback being gathered and used, as illustrated in Fig. 2.

Here the dotted lines represent information gathered about the interaction of pupils and learning environment, about the pupils and about the outcomes, both intended and unintended. What cannot be easily represented in a diagram is that this process is a cyclic one. Information on its own does not solve the crucial problem of matching which concerns deciding the next step which each pupil can and should take. But if the process of making a decision and gathering information about its effect is a cyclic one, then the optimum conditions can be approached through a series of approximations. The effect of gathering information in this way is also cumulative, helping not only the present situation but building up a store of knowledge about pupils and activities which can inform future decisions. Thus this concept of matching is as a dynamic process in which feedback plays an essential rôle.

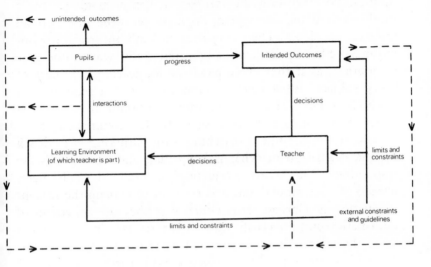

Fig.2

Most teachers will, hopefully, recognise this as something they already do, or attempt to do, but would not have found it necessary to analyse in this way. Analysis is necessary, however, if we wish to identify what kind of help teachers may need for matching to be improved. Teachers are required to make decisions about intended outcomes and so must be able to find help as to what lines of development are appropriate and what the points of this development are. This includes knowing, for example, that some ideas children will form would be described as 'wrong' by adult specialists, but are unavoidable steps in development because of children's limited experience and their ways of thinking. Having some idea of lines of progress which can be expected has to be supported by knowing how to foster progress; what methods, materials, activities are likely to be appropriate at each stage.

63

It has been stressed all along in this chapter that decisions about content are only part of the matter; methods and organisations are also important in providing learning opportunities. For too long the impression has been given that a single method and one type of organisation is the answer to all teaching problems. 'Discovery learning' and 'informal' organisation have been mistakenly advocated in this way at one time or another, as if they were panaceae for teaching all parts of every subject. What teachers need to have is a repertoire of methods and organisations, but most important, to know how to select the appropriate ones for particular circumstances.

Basic to the attempt at matching is the gathering of feedback for the evaluation of what is happening and how pupils are responding. The word 'evaluation' is used advisedly here, instead of 'assessment' and it is relevant to explain the reason. Evaluation is a broad term which describes the collection of information and the clarification of criteria used in judging and using the information. Assessment describes a range of methods which can be used for collecting information. Assessment implies some attempt to measure or to compare with a standard, but this need not be a fixed and widely used standard. Thus a remark made to a child such as 'good', either spoken or written, implies an assessment, often in terms of a standard which applies only to that child. A similar response by another child might bring forth a different remark, since the assessment might be against a different set of expectations for that pupil. The word assessment covers a range of methods, from the use of standardised tests to informal observation using child-based standards, as just mentioned [and see Chapter 3]. But there are other methods of gathering information than assessment. These others do not imply an attempt to summarise or measure; they can be best described as 'collection' or 'description'.

Taking samples of work, making notes describing behaviour, using recording techniques, are examples of these ways of gathering information. They do, of course, imply some selec-

helpful force where it starts in the school, involves teachers in the clarification of their intentions and the evaluation of how well these are implemented and leads to a dialogue with those outside the school who have the right to know what is happening. The negative effect on schools of accountability schemes comes when these are imposed from outside the schools, applying criteria which may not be shared by those inside. The 'back to basics' move had many contributing factors but one was certainly that schools were caught unable to give good answers to why a broad curriculum was better than a narrow one.

Responding to New Demands—Some Issues

These are only some of the directions from which there appear to be forces combining to emphasise the importance in teachers' work of evaluation and self-appraisal. The possibility of teachers being able to respond to more demands depends, however, on two crucial conditions; that time is made available and that teachers receive the help to acquire or sharpen the necessary skills. It is no use disguising that evaluation is time-consuming, particularly when first undertaken. Evaluation can also save time by enabling better informed decisions, but there has to be an initial outlay of effort before there is compensation for it. Similarly, there can be no denying that changes of attitude may well be needed; there is little point in gathering information unless there is the willingness to take note of it, to accept the criticism of existing practice which it often entails and to make changes.

What can be done to ease the problem of making time for the in-service courses that will be needed by some to acquire skills of evaluation, time for gathering information and, most important, time to reflect on it? The frustrating situation at present is that opportunities potentially exist, in falling rolls, to re-allocate a teacher's time. For economic reasons these opportunities are being missed and teachers have no chance to spend less of their working time in pupil contact. There seems little practical alternative at the moment to teachers spending some of their own time in reflection and discussion with colleagues. The educational reasons for this are put in strong words by Elliott (1979): 'A school that is reluctant to engage in an honest self-appraisal reveals a lack of genuine concern about the extent to which its policies are socially and educationally worthwhile.' Elliott also points out what the alternative is, that if schools do not evaluate themselves then others will do so from outside with the consequent loss of autonomy: 'Externally imposed evaluation systems are essentially the means of getting schools to comply with policies decided elsewhere.'

For all decisions, from the moment-to-moment ones aimed at matching activities to pupils to the ones at the level of policy which decide the broad framework of pupils' experiences, information is required. The techniques for collecting data are not complex nor do they require the services of experts, but teachers do need to know about them and especially how to choose relevant and efficient ones for particular purposes. The question then arises as to what kind of in-service education can provide the necessary help? We have learned much that is relevant in answering this question from the attempts to introduce new curriculum materials. When teachers have been presented with new *products* and told how to use them, the result has often been little or no real change of the kind intended. When involved in the *process* of examining what is lacking in existing practice and developing ways of improving it, then the innovation has been more likely to be implemented [see Chapter 10]. It is through involvement that the process of dissemination of new skills or materials reaches the point that Rudduck and Kelly (1976) described as 're-education'. When dissemination falls short of this point it fails to bring about real changes. Similarly, in disseminating the new skills necessary for evaluation it is not sufficient to communicate what techniques exist or to provide new ones, but rather to involve teachers in discussing the need for evaluation, analysing real problems and

seeing for themselves where certain techniques are appropriate. It was the experience of the 'Progress in Learning Science'
project which attempted to help with the process of matching,
that solutions produced by others were not seen as helpful by
teachers unless the thinking which had gone into them was
experienced at first hand (Harlen, 1977).

Finally, returning to the problem of helping with matching,
it may be that there is help which is required in those
curriculum areas where matching is less satisfactory over and
above making time and in-service courses available. It may be
that some of the other possible associated factors mentioned at
the beginning of this chapter should be examined. Pre-service
courses could themselves be evaluated to see if they provide an
adequate preparation for the demands on teachers, including
the skills required for self-appraisal and for decision-making at
various levels [see Chapter 9]. Not everything can be done at
the pre-service stage, however, and the whole professional
preparation and continued development of teachers would
benefit from a thorough examination of what is best attempted
in pre-service and what in in-service. The lack of co-ordination
between these is a waste of scarce time at both stages.

Further, we might re-examine the kind of help given to
teachers in the areas where their own knowledge is likely to be
patchy at best. Curriculum developers have frowned upon the
notion of 'structured' materials, preferring, for good theoretical reasons, to leave the decision about selecting and sequenc-
ing activities to teachers. But there are different kinds of
structure and not all lead to poor teaching. It is perhaps time to
be more open-minded about the value of different kinds of
materials. A degree of structure is helpful, both to teachers and
pupils, but what this degree is varies between individuals.
More work is necessary to discover how best to give the
amount of support which some teachers must have to function
with confidence and yet at the same time also provide the
flexibility for adaptation to the needs of individual pupils. All
this is to acknowledge that teachers are individuals, as are

pupils, and vary in their need of support. Matching is as relevant in helping teachers as it is in helping children.

References

Ashton, P., Kneen, P., Davies, F. and Holley, B. J., 1975, *The Aims of Primary Education: a Study of Teachers' Opinions.* Schools Council Research Series. London; Macmillan Education

Bennett, N., 1978, 'Surveyed from a shaky base'. *Times Educational Supplement* 3 Nov. 1978

Bloom, B. S., 1971, 'Affective consequences of school achievement'. In *Mastery Learning,* J. H. Block (Ed.). New York; Holt, Rinehart & Winston

Bruner, J. S., 1960, *The Process of Education.* New York; Vintage

C.A.C.E., 1967, *Children and their Primary Schools.* London; HMSO

Elliott, J., 1979, 'The case for school self-evaluation'. *Forum,* Autumn

Harlen, W., 1977, 'A stronger teacher role in curriculum development.' *Journal of Curriculum Studies,* Vol. 9 No. 1 May

Harlen, W., 1978, 'Evaluation and individual pupils'. In *Evaluation and the Teacher's Role,* W. Harlen (Ed.). Schools Council Research Series, London; Macmillan Education

Piaget, J., 1970, *Science of Education and the Psychology of the Child.* London; Longman

Rudduck, J. & Kelly, P. J., 1976, *The Dissemination of Curriculum Development.* Slough: NFER (European trend reports in educational research)

COMMUNITY AND DIVERSITY

6

Primary Education:
the multi-cultural context

Bev. Woodroffe

Awareness

Many of us find it difficult to make any real sense of the idea that Britain is a multi-cultural society. It is certainly easier for us to grasp that Britain has problems of race relations. It is easier, too, to understand that our future in relation to world politics demands both knowledge and understanding of not only the 'first' and 'second' worlds but also the 'third world'. The increasing impact of Islam and the centrality of Africa in current political events are pointers to the new awareness that is demanded. The importance of such issues obliges us to look at how the educational system is preparing young people for this new awareness. It obliges us, also, to question the educational arrangements we make for young people of different races, ethnic and cultural groups to learn and work alongside one another. We need to direct our attention not only to the inner cities which are multi-ethnic and multi-cultural but also throughout Britain.

It is possible, and easy, to assert the need for this approach but it is necessary to return to the question of why we find it so difficult to make sense of the idea of a multi-cultural society. We need to look at our own formal education and the formative experiences that have shaped our attitudes, awareness (or lack of it) and our understanding. Whatever our age, we almost certainly followed a formal curriculum that was ethnocentric and European-based; the hidden curriculum for those of us over thirty either ignored much of the rest of the world or subtly placed low value or ridicule upon it. Remember the messages of books, comics, jokes and fantastic tales of 'fuzzy-wuzzies' or exotic but inefficient 'Asiatics'. More recently the hidden curriculum has dwelt upon the problems, disadvantages and dangers of being from the 'third world'—a black teacher told me recently of his amazement on being asked at an interview what he thought of Idi Amin. The issue that we have to confront is how do we, within the educational system, prepare young people to understand, make sense of, and develop a multi-cultural society in a shrinking world. Crucially we need to develop a positive approach to the strengths of difference: difference in culture, in experience, in perception and in values which our former experience of imperialism and colonialism has eroded and distorted.

That distortion has led to racism becoming embedded in our society. It is impossible, and would be wrong, to try to divorce emotion from the question of racism, the main plank of which is an assumption of one's own race, whatever we mean by that, being in nearly all ways superior to others. Yet if we are to develop education within a multi-cultural context, we have to be objective, logical *and* imaginative. We must recognise that we are products of a certain sort of society and that those of us with British backgrounds share a history with those whose backgrounds lie in what was once the British Empire. Unless we start from this point, our responses in education are likely to contain the same distortions as in the past.

It is essential also to be quite clear of our response up to the present time, for though we have responded at times effectively, more often we have not, and where our response has been ill-judged it has still become built into our educational arrangements. The Plowden Report (1967) contains a chapter

74

entitled 'Children of Immigrants' whose essential focus of concern can best be understood by its recommendations:

(i) Colleges, institutes of education and local education authorities should expand opportunities through initial and in-service courses for some teachers to train in teaching English to immigrants and to increase their knowledge of the background from which children come.

(ii) Work already started on the development of suitable materials and methods for teaching English to immigrants should continue and be expanded.

(iii) Dispersal may be necessary but language and other difficulties should be the criteria employed.

(iv) There should be an expansion of remedial courses in spoken English for immigrant teachers.

(v) Schools with special language problems . . . should be generously staffed: further experiments might be made in the use of student volunteers.

This focus on special needs is consistent with current thinking and shows a proper concern with *one* aspect within the multi-cultural context. What is significant, though, are the statements in the report that 'the purposes of the various measures we have discussed should be to eliminate, not perpetuate, the need for them' and 'special measures inevitably identify children as "different" and their duration should be as brief as possible'. The report hopes that immigrant children will be quickly 'absorbed into the native population'. I find it interesting that elsewhere in the same report suggestions are made both about broadening the curriculum and checking books for bias and distortion through stereotypes. The lack of consistent thinking and true understanding of the multi-cultural context and its implications throws up inconsistent responses but more worryingly suggests by the term absorption the idea that a process of assimilation will make us all 'British' and thus wipe away the differences for which special measures are inconveniently required.

The years between the Plowden Report and the HMI primary survey may be characterised by, on the one hand, a growing number of specialist reports by bodies such as the Parliamentary Select Committee on Immigration and Race Relations and by organisations representing minority group opinion, which continually to a greater or lesser degree question the approach as expressed in Plowden, and on the other hand the partial reference which is allowed to appear in major educational documents such as the Bullock Report. *Primary Education in England* (1978) attaches importance to the arrangements and approaches to second language learners and notes some expansion of the curriculum in relation to the multi-cultural context. Amongst the recommendations is stated: 'More might be done to make all children aware of other beliefs and to extend their understanding of the multi-cultural nature of contemporary society. In the course of work on these and other matters, children acquire information and learn to respond imaginatively to what they see, hear and otherwise experience'. Close scrutiny of the report does indicate a proper shift in thinking, yet, as I believe the extract shows, there is no *clear* intention to place the issue centrally into the debate concerning primary education nor therefore to give firm leadership. 'More *might* be done'!

Aims and Issues

What can be done? What needs to be done? First and foremost, we need to recognise the centrality of the issues presented by the multi-cultural context. They are central because they add a dimension to all aspects of the thinking of those engaged in primary education. We need to spell out the aims of multi-ethnic education along the lines of those outlined by the Inner London Education Authority in a recent report:

a to prepare all pupils and students to live and work harmoniously and with equality of opportunity in that society;

b to build upon the strengths of cultural diversity in that society;

c to define and combat racism and the discriminatory practices to which it gives rise; and

d to meet appropriately and effectively the particular needs of all people, having regard to their ethnic, cultural, linguistic or historical attachment.

In order to respond effectively to aims such as these we need to follow a process of identification, review of our policies and practices, development and consolidation. For example, racism affects the young child both in Harwich and in Handsworth, yet our detailed response will need to take in the difference of experience of these two areas. To put it as succinctly as I can, we need two sorts of checklist. One will be addressed to the issues to which primary education should respond; the other will be addressed to the aspects of primary education where the responses can be most appropriately developed.

In discussion of multi-cultural education these issues have been somewhat confused because of the settlement patterns of ethnic minorities in the inner city areas. Multi-cultural education has become synonymous with education in the inner cities, itself heavily overlaid with ideas of disadvantage. There is no doubt that the initial difficulties that follow immigration have been compounded by discrimination tabulated, for example, in PEP reports and recognised by Parliament with the resultant 1976 Race Relations Act. Such discrimination, allied to a widespread belief that we should 'treat all children alike' (usually meaning like a stereotype of white indigenous children) has led to inappropriate pragmatic responses. It is essential, if we are to formulate appropriate policies, that this confusion is untangled. The issues to isolate are these:

a assisting children to a self-identity in a multi-cultural society; this is of equal importance to indigenous white British children as to others;

b creating the basis of a wider world understanding through broader cultural and historical sources and experience;
c combating racist ideas which are often supported in education by a narrow approach to values and by the development of stereotypes;
d fostering the development of inter-group relations through the ethos of the school, curriculum and other activities;
e introducing the idea of linguistic diversity, in the world, in Europe, in this country.

As I have indicated earlier, these issues are national issues and, we must remember, European ones. If we could only respond effectively, we would destroy many of the disadvantages placed upon learners from minority ethnic groups and so be able to identify the particular needs that relate to a learner's 'ethnic, cultural, linguistic or historical attachment'.

Policies

Policy implications exist at three levels: national, local authority and school. At national level there has been an indication of such policy in the Green Paper, *Education in Schools* (1977):

> 'Our society is a multicultural, multiracial one, and the curriculum should reflect a sympathetic understanding of the different cultures and races that now make up our society. We also live in a complex, interdependent world, and many of our problems in Britain require international solutions. The curriculum should therefore reflect our need to know about and understand other countries.'

It is important that such 'signals', as the Minister of Education in the Netherlands, Dr Pias, recently put it, be made regularly and consistently by the government and the DES and that these signals permeate thinking, presentation and day-to-day work. There is a need to place emphasis more widely through national surveys, curriculum guidance and reports. It is necessary to continue this emphasis within the work of the Schools Council, in the development of policies in relation to initial and in-service training and in the production of resources for teaching and learning. A more coherent approach to research and development drawing upon the resources of institutions of higher education, the NFER and funding bodies, such as the SSRC, needs to be developed.

At local authority level there needs equally to be a signalling of the centrality of multi-ethnic issues. An overall policy strategy should concentrate upon development with clear administrative implications. A key factor is the creation of time for teachers, with advisers, to plan, develop, test and evaluate methods and approaches; successful development then requires proper means for dissemination. One possible model is exemplified in the development of the 'Reading through Understanding' project within the ILEA. Here an initial hypothesis that dialect used at home interfered with the young child's acquisition of literacy was found not to be valid. Through research and observation of children in the classroom it became apparent that children of Caribbean origin were adversely affected by the overwhelmingly 'White English' content of materials and by the lower expectation and attitude of teachers towards them as learners and readers. Strongly concentrating on cooperation with classroom teachers, the project team developed materials at initial reading level, top infant and lower junior, top junior and lower secondary, which were set in a multi-cultural British locality, drew upon folk tales from other cultures especially African and Caribbean, and included stories of people with fine qualities who came from different parts of the world. These materials, and most importantly the approach and method, have now become the central point for an in-service training programme for primary teachers. It needs to be stressed that a key part of the development was the central involvement in the team of a teacher of Caribbean origin whose knowledge and experience were essential. At local authority level, then, in addition to a clear administrative policy, advisers should develop in-service training, methods of guidance and the support and dissemination of good practice, drawing into

COMMUNITY AND DIVERSITY

this process at all levels people with the necessary background, experience and, where possible, training.

At school level the headteacher has a most positive rôle to play in bringing the issues into the whole life of the school. A policy and an approach to its development need to be made, if a genuine shift in the learning experiences offered all children is to be achieved. In many schools at the moment one or more teachers are developing their own approaches which could be translated into a constant factor throughout the school.

There are many opportunities which could be taken by teachers, given the support and coordination provided by a policy. For example, stories could be used to open up the multi-cultural world for young children. By choosing stories with varied settings teachers could begin to open up for the child similar experiences shaped in different settings—universal themes in varying contexts. By their selection of stories to be told, looked at and, in time, read by the child, and their implicit acceptance of values in other societies, teachers could lay the foundation of important attitudes. They could destroy for the next generation the penetratingly harmful stereotypes that shaped their own attitudes and values. Allied to this could be an introduction to the vitally important theme of man's adaptation to his physical, social and economic environment. Very simply, the location and structure of a house in a tropical country in relation to the demands of the climate could be understood and enjoyed by a young child and could thereby provide a sensible base for the more complex learning of later years. This approach could be extended so young children are introduced to the variety of family structures, social customs, social organisation, faiths and, indeed, to the bases on which Jerome Bruner built his middle years curriculum, *Man: A Course of Study*.

Of course, I am advocating a policy of permeation throughout the primary curriculum, a permeation which could have marked effects on both teacher and taught. One more example: just think of the idea that those of us whose families have lived in Britain for generations share a history with the countries of the Commonwealth, and that that shared history involves the influence of both the coloniser and the colonised. This could lead teachers to question the interpretation of the history they were given and to seek out the 'hidden' history. After that, could they continue an approach which gave a special value to the technological achievements, the artistic expression and indeed the ethos of Western society, whilst by subtle implication it devalued that of other societies? It is by teasing out meaningful reference points for young children in primary classrooms that teachers could begin to prepare the ground upon which new awareness is forged.

Relocation

In conclusion, it is perhaps appropriate to recognise that a major national acceptance of the mutli-cultural dimension in education may not be forthcoming, though hopefully the government enquiry into multi-cultural education might take on significance. Whether such an acceptance and a corresponding shift of policy and practice occur or not, the relocation of individuals' perspectives can occur, will occur and is occurring all the time. It is not an exaggeration to say that a person achieves a real release by becoming free of misconceptions and the results of racism and ethnocentrism. The primary teacher, the adviser, the inspector, the administrator and the curriculum developer can and need to share the same perspective. As I have stressed earlier, education in and for a multi-cultural society needs at all levels the full participation of members of all ethnic and cultural groups.

References

Central Advisory Council for Education (England), 1967, *Children and their Primary Schools*, London, HMSO

COMMUNITY AND DIVERSITY

Department of Education and Science, 1977, *Education in Schools: a consultative document*, London, HMSO

Department of Education and Science, 1978, *Primary Education in England: A survey by HM Inspectors of Schools*, London, HMSO

82

7

The School, Parents and Local Community

Joan Sallis

The fact that I, a parent never professionally involved in education, have been invited to write this chapter is in a sense a justification for its inclusion in the book, for it reflects the growing acceptance of the contribution made by a child's home and social environment to his success at school. It is even more encouraging that in in-service training generally it is more and more common to find a slot for 'home and community' in studies of a wide range of teaching problems and skills. Tolerant—or masochistic!—people continue to give me an open invitation to be cheeky to 'Sir' on such occasions; to write, metaphorically speaking, on the school walls.

Perhaps, however, truisms do not rise to the top quite as fast as cream on the milk. It is less encouraging that in its background paper for the 'Great Debate', which was after all concerned with the way schools were responding to the needs of society, the DES in their title referred to '*our* children' (my italics) without as far as I could see any reference at all to parents in the text. More recently (1978), and with painful relevance, the Inspectorate, in their introduction to *Primary Education in England*, admit that the reader will find no reference to the wider links between home and school. While acknowledging the importance of such links, HMI maintain apparently that it is possible to exclude them from a survey of 'the work done in institutions and classrooms', a survey which presumably is therefore concerned to judge how far the latter

83

are meeting the needs of the whole child and all our whole children. I hope to show that in one respect this omission gravely reduces the value of a survey which in other respects is a great encouragement to those who are trying to keep the whole child in mind.

My theme is that while teachers, and those training teachers, have become very committed to, and perceptive about, the ideal of the shared responsibility of school and home, those in high places who provide the framework within which teachers operate, do not always show the same perception and commitment. The DES, whose Secretary of State is charged in the 1944 Act 'to promote the education of the people of England and Wales' still has no place in its organisation concerned with home-links, parents' problems, the rôle of the community. It also strikes me that the LEA is in a strangely illogical position: if the LEA is responsible for the effectiveness of the local schools, and that effectiveness can be nothing more than the sum of a very large number of individual relationships, and every survey shows that home support is the largest single variable in the effectiveness of those individual relationships, why is there no formal, organised acceptance of responsibility by the LEA for securing a higher level of home support, presumably our most under-exploited resource? It seems that it will take a very long time for this nation to desire for all children what a 'wise' and 'good' parent desires for his own child—you may have to ask my children's grandchildren how long.

I have implied that primary teachers, whom I increasingly find the most inspiring group of people I meet, understand very well the implications of researches into the importance of home links. I am also sure that many of them feel inadequately supported in acting on that understanding, under-resourced to follow its logic through, defeated sometimes by the size of the task. In this situation, knowing what the task is can sometimes be small comfort. They know that a lot of rubbish is talked about 'parental involvement', for they know that the battle, if it ever was a battle, for 'wise' and 'good' parents to express their aspirations, was over long ago. They know that from Cranleigh to Alderley Edge, from Solihull to Harrow-on-the Hill—pleasant places chosen at random—there isn't any doubt about the splendid support given by the PTA, the fine attendance at open evenings, the help parents give not only to their own children, under the school's kindly guidance, but in the school repairing library books and raising money for extras.

When teachers invite me to their conferences, I always say that I haven't come all that way to talk about these admirable, but increasingly uncontroversial and only marginally relevant, aspects of home-school co-operation. For I know as well as they do that in the happily open and informal atmosphere of many of today's primary schools, parents whose own educational experience has been successful and whose lives since school have increased rather than reduced their confidence, have little difficulty in understanding what the school aims at, in supporting both the school and their own child's progress through it and in voicing their concerns and hopes. Their aspirations are to a large extent built into the system anyway. What worries teachers is the crying need of children whose homes have low aspirations or none, whose parents have very limited opportunity to be 'wise' or 'good', whose families often wrestle with problems so great that it seems almost an impertinence to expect any more of them. Teachers are concerned that the parents of these children still feel intimidated by schools, often desperately want to know how they can help their children to do well, and *are*, if only vaguely, aware of inadequacies as parents which they feel helpless alone to remedy.

While we try ardently, if with limited success, to iron out some of the more obvious inequalities of the education process, there are some gaps we may even be widening. We bring into sharper and sharper relief the most intractable injustice of all—that of inequalities in parenting. For although parents have a very solemn duty, enshrined in the law and

85

underlined by every piece of research, to see that their children receive a suitable education, this is virtually the only *positive* requirement imposed on parents once they have registered the birth of their child. There is no compulsion, and only limited assistance, to be a 'good' parent. Even in the days when they were given free milk and orange juice, no law kept the milk out of grandma's tea or the orange juice out of her gin; no law could say more than that you shall not abuse or wilfully neglect your child. You were even in those days free to choose Coke instead of orange juice and are still free to choose comics rather than Ladybird books. Yet the very existence of a public education system is an unspoken acceptance of the right of children to rise above the aspirations of their parents. Hundreds of thousands of teachers are struggling to give effect to that right. All I really want to ask in this chapter is whether we have ever been serious enough about providing the means for them to do so.

Appropriately, we talk a good deal about the problems arising from a multi-racial society. Yet long before our schools became so conspicuously multi-racial, there were differences between what children brought to the education process as great as if they had come from different planets, never mind different continents. I am speaking of the gulf between those whose homes are at one extreme without joy or order, without conversation, without even nursery rhymes, and at the other, children who enjoy music lessons, nature walks, visits to the Toy Museum, Sunday breakfast with the colour supplements and sophisticated family repartee. I once saw some writing by children in one class about how they had spent a day. One said

'We played a trio before breakfast and in the morning my dad took me out to find leaves for my project. We visited some friends with a big collection of costume dolls and their mum helped us make some clothes for them. In bed I read some more of "The Lion, the Witch and the Wardrobe".'

The other said,

> 'My dad was in a bad temper because he'd been on nights, and he was mad with me for messing about. I went over my Nan's and she gave me money to buy a comic and some crisps. When I'd finished them I messed about in her road. It was boring, and I was pleased when it was time to come in and watch "Dr Who".'

At this point, having pointed the starkest contrast, I come to something which worries me about the primary survey. In the conclusions it makes on 'match', which contain some inevitably very political points about meeting the needs of the most able, it relies heavily on the teacher's classification of the children into three groups by capability. How, especially with the younger groups, can a teacher possibly allow for such extreme difference in social input? How can she be sure that she is not doing a double injustice by having low expectations of children who present to the outside world merely the low expectations of their homes? Teachers of younger children are busy trying to bridge some of these gaps, too busy often, even if they think it appropriate, to make such judgments, as they put all their skill into identifying and treating the most crying deficiencies in a child's experience. Children start school in all shades of grey, from the obviously academic little boy who talks like an old man but can't actually manage his flies, to the one who can give you change from £5 but doesn't speak in sentences. In the two years which follow, the infant teacher is busy trying to meet the needs of both, individually. No teacher I have spoken to is happy about this aspect of the survey or its exclusion of those home link[s]

introduction pays lip service. [A]

judgment they could have made

with sufficient accuracy such thi[n]

eagerness to put the hand up, s[o]

convey, a background of clear l[a]

well-directed play, and all the co[

This omission, and this technique, greatly reduce for me the impact of the survey. A pity, since I so heartily welcome what it does in other ways for the whole-child ideal. It gives us much-needed ammunition [as Norman Thomas indicates] by showing that performance in basics is not in inverse proportion to curriculum breadth, just the opposite. This, popularly presented, could do so much for home and community support of what the school is doing, and at the same time strike a blow against all those insidious critics of education who don't want us to waste non-basic education on those who 'can't appreciate it', i.e. need it most.

In some ways the gross inequalities in home input of which I have spoken could get worse. Falling rolls could, ill-managed, segregate the strong and cruelly isolate the weak. There are already whole schools in which teachers work twice as hard to achieve half as much. Are we to increase their number? It will all be done in the name of brave ideals like choice and freedom in an outbreak of consumerism-rampant such as we have never seen. It could easily be the means of concentrating all the parents who make a fuss in the few schools without problems, and providing for the rest a wholesome cheap alternative. Market forces are invoked as a desirable ideal, but the analogy is cruelly inept, for parents do not consume education. They are equally responsible with the school for its success, they are part of their schools and they change them. The heart of my theme is that children's chances are still intolerably dependent on how well-equipped their parents are to support them, on their capacity to understand what is needed, and on the confidence with which they deal with schools. To make choice of school entirely dependent on parents' aspirations, without a good deal of conscious effort to compensate for low home input, can only widen the quality gap. Most of the educational politicians—with a small as well as large 'P'—are busy at ... with massive irrelevancies. The real question, how ... ies in home and community input can be lessened, ... a thought. How, in short, to make a reality of the *mutual* accountability of school and home for a shared process.

It doesn't help that our sensitivity in talking about differences in the quality of parenting is equalled only by our embarrassment in discussing differences of teacher quality. Indeed, one exacerbates the other. From these sensitivities, only the child must suffer. One of my remedies is the growth of habits of much greater frankness about both. Teachers might like to say that in many homes without real problems, education is still given too low a priority, that somebody would sooner watch television than provide quiet, sooner go to football than go and collect those seed-pods. They say that many homes expect schools to do what they are neither willing nor able to do themselves: simple things like saying 'No'. Parents, however, will refuse to be lectured about such things while they do not feel accepted as equals in school. For some time people in education have been searching for a means of introducing a little formality into the shared responsibility idea: contracts, covenants, and the like. The Taylor Committee (1977) went as far as we probably yet can by suggesting that enrolment at school be invested with a little formality through a letter containing promises about the ways the school would involve parents and suggestions about how parents could be more helpfully involved.

The parent group on that committee, joined by four others, also thought that it was essential to enshrine in law the right of the *individual* parent to information relevant to his statutory duty. For another thing which doesn't help is that all our laudable attempts to improve *collective* accountabilities—more rights for PTAs, parents on governing bodies, etc.—can, if pursued alone, exclude people. When I go to one of those happy welcoming schools where the head calls the PTA chairman 'Daphne', I always wonder treacherously whether such cosiness makes anybody feel excluded. Of course we must pursue better corporate communication, but at the same time we have to ensure that the individual feels dignified, important, and at the end of the day, endowed with access to the school in his own right, not through somebody else.

I hope it has been clear that, while I think the work our many good schools are doing to involve *all* parents in their affairs must continue, I also think the time has come for a little more help from on high. Recognition by central and local government that it is an essential part of their statutory duties to create frameworks of rights, responsibilities and good communication must come. I should also like to see more research sponsored into which methods of involving parents and neighbourhoods with schools have proved most successful, so as to spread good practice and help those who *want* to do it better. I should like to see a much greater frankness with parents and the public about the educational problems of *whole* schools, *whole* communities. If we are selfish in pursuing our own children's interests, it is largely because we have never had the encouragement or the right to be otherwise. Only by a conscious effort can the goodwill of 'wise' and 'good' parents be enlisted to improve the chances of the *children* who have not this greatest of all privileges.

Finally, and most important, comes the widest gap of all in the logic of our position. We accept that schools alone cannot right all the wrongs of society, and that where there are social and economic problems they will not only be reflected in schools: they will rock them to their foundations. It must thus be accepted that home input is the greatest inequality children suffer in their education; every piece of evidence suggests that it is the greatest single variable. If, then, we are really serious about equal opportunity for children, how can we possibly justify doing so little to compensate the low-input school, and the child from the low-input home? Yes, we have our SPA areas and a modest degree of positive discrimination, but in relation to the need, what we have done so far is just children's games. Enrichment is talked about, rarely financed. In an increasingly buyers' market, the cruel inequalities will only increase if we do not support as a nation that the children of 'good' and 'wise' parents are all right, thank you. The desperate need is to enlist the concern and humanity of such parents in the interests of the rest, and find the means of giving more to those to whom life has given less.

References

Department of Education and Science, 1977, *Educating Our Children: Four subjects for debate*, London, DES

Department of Education and Science/Welsh Office, 1977, *A New Partnership for Our Schools*, (The Taylor Report), London, HMSO

Department of Education and Science, 1978, *Primary Education in England: A survey by HM Inspectors of Schools*, London, HMSO

8

Responding to Diversity: children with special needs

George Cooke

All children are unique individuals and therefore all children are to some extent 'special'. Over the years, the primary schools in this country have more and more recognised and responded to the need to 'cater for difference'. It may be argued that some trends in social attitudes and educational thought and practice (particularly at the secondary stage) have been pulling in the opposite direction; yet very few teachers (or parents) of primary age children would dispute the proposition that the 'average child' does not really exist outside the realms of statistics and market research. Nevertheless, the *idea* of the average child, like the idea of the man on the Clapham bus, remains a convenient abstraction for education because it enables attention to be focused not only on those needs and aspirations which are common to all children but also on those children who form the majority of the school population and for whom a fairly standard provision is likely to produce a reasonably successful result. It is necessary in most human affairs to strike some sort of balance between catering for difference and exploiting the common ground, and we can accept easily enough, without it being much help to us, that we are all in some important ways the same, and in other important ways different. The key point for education is that some children are much more obviously and significantly 'different' than others, and problems arise when the *nature* and *degree* of the differences are so great that they cannot adequately be catered for within the ordinary or 'mainstream' system without special measures. It is on this basis that we commonly identify, for good practical reasons, those children whom we describe as 'exceptional'. They fall into two main groups: those who are exceptionally gifted or outstanding; and those who have special educational needs because of handicap, disability, disorder, disadvantage or learning and other difficulties. The crucial issues for the education of these children are first how to identify them and then how to provide more adequately for them.

The Plowden Report (1967), whilst endorsing a great deal of existing 'best practice' in primary education, strongly urged the need for positive discrimination in favour of children suffering from educational and social disadvantages. The Warnock Report (1978) put forward a new concept of 'special educational need' embracing not only those children who have traditionally been described as 'handicapped' but also those (generally in ordinary schools) who have milder, but nevertheless serious, learning or emotional or behavioural difficulties. The case for better provision for these children (up to one in five of the school population, says Warnock) is a compelling one, not only in terms of individual fulfilment and human dignity but also in terms of economic advantage and social cohesion within the community as a whole.

During the last decade or so there have also been signs of increasing concern about the inadequacy of the educational response to the needs of exceptionally gifted children. The foundation of the National Association for Gifted Children in 1966 was an expression of a deeply-felt anxiety, and despite a good deal of attention since then by HM Inspectorate, the Schools Council, many LEAs and a large number of teachers, *Primary Education in England: A survey by HM Inspectors of Schools* (1978) still reveals disturbing evidence of very able children who are under-achieving because they are insufficiently stretched.

Thus, the generalised worries about standards and accountability throughout the education system (exemplified in the Great Debate of 1976–77) are matched by more specific dissatisfaction about what is being done (or, more accurately, not being done) for those children who have exceptional gifts or exceptional problems. There are quite a number of people who feel that our current family and community standards, teacher attitudes and expectations, and school organisation and resources, may be militating quite severely *against* the interests of exceptional children of all kinds. The present concern, therefore, is timely—but it should not be taken as evidence of problems unique to this country. The same arguments, with very similar degrees of heat and light, are taking place throughout the countries of the Western world. It is not without significance that the first World Congress of the Council for Exceptional Children held at Stirling University in 1978 attracted (to the surprise and somewhat to the embarrassment of its organisers) three or four times the number of delegates originally expected.

If our schools are to improve their contribution and their reputation in the years ahead, they must not only turn the nation's present mood of doubt and dissatisfaction to their advantage, but also be prepared to seize future opportunities as they present themselves. It seems pretty clear that, in the early 1980s at any rate, extra resources will be hard to come by in the public sector, and if education does not make its own claim vigorously and effectively, it will inevitably go by default or succumb to the rival claims of other caring services with equally, and in their view more, urgent needs. The arguments for education are available and powerful—but they must be *used*. If, for example, the teachers in 'mainstream' primary and secondary schools do not understand or appreciate the significance of the Warnock Report's recommendations for them, they will in a very real sense prejudice their own, as well as their pupils', prospects for growth and development. We are surely not required to assume that our present economic and financial difficulties will continue unabated for the rest of this

94

century, but even if they do, much can be done *without* a vast injection of new financial resources. Changes in ideas, attitudes and expectations, changes in methods of working and working together, are always, in the final analysis, more potent influences on the *quality* of the education service than increased expenditure, and the latter is only really justified if it contributes towards the former. This is not to say that money is not important or that more money will not be required. It is simply to say that more money will be hard to get and, if we need it, we shall have to justify our need very forcefully and persuasively. Yet, despite all this, the next decade or so *will* present a unique opportunity for worthwhile improvements if we get our aims and priorities (and our public relations!) right. Politicians being what they are, we can be assured that, whatever the economic climate, *some* more money *will* be available for initiatives which can be shown to be educationally important, socially desirable *and* politically expedient. Moreover, the certain dramatic fall in the total child population in school in the 1980s *will* create, alongside many grave problems in the 'management of contraction', real opportunities for re-assessment of priorities and redeployment of resources, particularly in the fields of teacher employment and professional in-service training [as illustrated by Chapters 9, 10 and 14].

How should all this affect our attitudes towards exceptional children of all kinds? If in recent years we have failed adequately to discharge our obligations to them, our failure is surely in part due to lack of knowledge, understanding and skill (we are human and fallible, and all education is to some extent a story of failure). But it is also surely in part due to the ground-swell of professional, political and public opinion against any form of segregation or élitism, anything that unduly emphasises difference or is educationally and socially 'divisive'. The primary schools, whatever their internal organisation, have always been comprehensive in their intakes and have escaped the prolonged and often bitter battles associated

95

with the comprehensive reorganisation of secondary schools. For that reason they have, fortunately, been able to concentrate much more on children and less on systems and structures. But we now face a future in which, whatever the political twists and turns, all our primary schools and the vast majority of our secondary schools will clearly be comprehensive in organisation, and it is time to look again at the challenge presented to an essentially comprehensive system by the needs of exceptional children. *Can* the ordinary (comprehensive) schools cope adequately with their 'normal' resources, or do they need additional special resources, specialist support services and/or separate provision in highly specialised institutions? And if something extra *is* needed, how much of what kind and where? The issues are essentially the same whether we are talking about gifted children or children with special educational needs in Warnock terms. And the answer, in terms of the world-wide debate on 'integration', 'mainstreaming' or 'normalisation' can never properly, in my view, be plain black or white. Maximum integration—yes: total integration—no! If it is right (as I believe it is) to make very special, separate provision for *some* very severely handicapped or disturbed children, or for *some* children who have exceptional gifts in music or dancing, then the *principle* of 'total integration' is breached and the only important questions left are where the right balance lies, how far and under what conditions integration can be achieved successfully, how far and under what conditions separate specialist provision is necessary in the interests of the exceptional child, other children and the community.

It is interesting, in the wider context of exceptional children of all kinds and bearing in mind that the Warnock Committee explicitly excluded from its consideration highly gifted children unless they had emotional or behavioural problems, to look at the Warnock definitions of the aims of education and of special educational need and provision. Warnock (para. 1.4) says that the goals of education are:

'twofold, different from each other, but by no means incompatible. They are, first, to enlarge a child's knowledge, experience and imaginative understanding, and thus his awareness of moral values and capacity for enjoyment; and secondly, to enable him to enter the world after formal education is over as an active participant in society and a responsible contributor to it, capable of achieving as much independence as possible'.

These goals, argues Warnock, are the *same* for all children, but the progress made towards them is very different—fast, far and relatively easy for some—slow, painful and inevitably limited for others.

Warnock (para. 3.19) defines 'special educational need' in broad terms as a need for 'one or more of the following:

(i) the provision of special means of access to the curriculum through specialist equipment, facilities or resources, modification of the physical environment or specialist teaching techniques;
(ii) the provision of a special or modified curriculum;
(iii) particular attention to the social structure and emotional climate in which education takes place'.

Similarly, Warnock (para. 3.40) defines 'special educational provision' in terms of 'one or more of three criteria:

(i) effective access on a full or part-time basis to teachers with appropriate qualifications or substantial experience or both;
(ii) effective access on a full or part-time basis to other professionals with appropriate training; and
(iii) an educational and physical environment with the necessary aids, equipment and resources appropriate to the child's special needs'.

Though not aimed at gifted children, those definitions will, I think, serve pretty well for them also, and they apply equally

97

to all forms of 'special education' wherever it is provided—or educational opportunities provided outside the formal school environment altogether (from hospital and home tuition to specially organised 'enrichment' experiences in a non-school setting).

What does all this mean for the future development of our primary schools? It certainly does *not* mean wholesale rejection of all the immensely worthwhile and exciting developments that have taken place, to greater or less degree, in many of our primary schools since the 1939–45 war. The world-wide admiration of the best features of British primary education has been well earned and should not lightly be thrown away. What it *does* mean is that we must take a hard, critical look at our existing ways of doing things, and change the emphasis, if not the whole direction, of *some* of our ideas and activities. It means that central government, LEAs, schools, teacher education institutes, individual teachers and a number of other professionals must think again and take deliberate, conscious decisions on a wide range of very difficult questions. There are no easy or final answers. If there were, they would have been identified years ago. The important thing is that there should be more general recognition that the questions need to be asked, and a greater willingness to tackle them in new and imaginative ways.

The final sentence of the Warnock Report refers to 'those changes in attitude which are essential if our aims are to be fully realised', and the essential condition for attitudinal change is greater *awareness* of the needs of exceptional children and of the resources at our disposal to meet them. When we *know* more, we are more able and more ready to *do* more. There is still much ill-founded prejudice, even amongst professionals, about exceptional children; for example, there is a widespread belief that most exceptionally gifted children are spoiled or immature or 'difficult'; and there is an equally persistent belief that serious handicap in one area means general disability in all. It will be a good start if those and similar myths can be laid to rest forever.

More specifically we need, at various levels of decision-making, to tackle the following questions, *inter alia:*

(i) How far is there a continuing need for, and what kind of provision should be made in separate 'special' schools and units which are *not* integrated parts of ordinary 'mainstream' schools? The Warnock Committee was quite clear that there *would* be a continuing need of this kind for some of 'their' children, and some people still argue strongly for separate provision for highly gifted children on a selective basis in fields other than the creative arts.

(ii) Where provision for exceptional children is made in ordinary 'mainstream' schools, how much 'segregation' is still necessary or desirable within the school for different children in different circumstances? How much separate class/group provision, how much streaming or setting, how much 'withdrawal', how much specialist intervention and of what kind? How is all this best reconciled with the need to 'integrate' exceptional children as far as possible into the *whole* life and work of the ordinary school?

(iii) To what extent is the capacity of the ordinary school to respond effectively to the needs of exceptional children determined by 'internal' factors like leadership and staff morale, school organisation, attitudes to social responsibility and discipline, curricular aims and content, teacher deployment and development—or to 'external' factors like teacher supply and training, allocations of resources, advisory and specialist support services?

(iv) What resources, and especially what *teacher* resources, do we *really* need in a period of falling rolls and how can we make better use of the resources we have?

(v) How best can the highly specialised knowledge and experience of teachers in 'special' schools be made more generally available for the benefit of the whole education service?

(vi) How can we best exploit and develop special expertise among primary teachers generally? If (as most people seem to agree) primary age children need the continuity and stability provided by a class teacher in a class group, can we—through initial and in-service training, staff development programmes and school organisation—make more effective use of 'ordinary' class teachers as 'specialists in the primary school'—as HM Inspectors would like? Do we need, as Butcher and Dawkins (1979) have argued, 'a system of working which will enable each teacher to contribute to the school's work both as a general class teacher and by providing the school as a whole with expertise in one particular field'?

(vii) How far do we need specialist teachers with allocated special responsibilities in primary schools and for what purposes? How, bearing in mind that HM Inspectors found that 'the great majority of teachers with special curricular responsibilities had little influence on the work of other teachers', can the contribution of designated specialist teachers be made more effective? Do all primary schools need an appointed or visiting 'Warnock' specialist teacher? If so, are the Warnock recommendations for specialist in-service training right, and how can they be implemented most quickly and effectively? How best can such a specialist teacher exercise an influence throughout the whole school?

(viii) Do all general class teachers need—as Warnock suggests—short 'awareness' courses to give them a more sensitive understanding of special educational needs, and above all to help them to know when and what kind of specialist help to seek and how to get it? If so, what should be the content of these short courses; in what way(s) can they best be organised; how and how soon can a nationwide programme of such courses be mounted effectively?

(ix) Assuming (rightly, surely) that teachers in primary

schools need and would welcome *some* further help from 'outside' professional specialists in meeting the needs of exceptional children, what specialist support services are most needed and in what circumstances? How can maximum co-operation between professionals of different disciplines be developed?

(x) How, bearing in mind that the problems of exceptional children are most easily resolved if tackled early and consistently, can we improve our methods of ensuring the earliest possible identification, assessment and help for children with special needs?

(xi) When, and by what criteria, should an ordinary school staff conclude that a particular child's special educational needs cannot adequately be met within the school's resources (even with extra specialist help) and initiate procedures for placement in a 'special' school or unit?

(xii) What are the implications of better provision for exceptional children in terms of pupil-teacher ratios; mixed ability teaching; 'vertical' and 'horizontal' groupings; individual, group and class teaching; 'didactic' and 'exploratory' teaching methods?

(xiii) Is the curriculum broad enough, rich enough and challenging enough for exceptional children? Is it really up-to-date and adequately thought through? Does it positively encourage high expectation and achievement? Are the books and other resource materials in use really appropriate and the best that are available or can be produced?

(xiv) How far do exceptional children need special arrangements for 'enrichment' experiences within or outside the normal curriculum? What special resources can be made available to provide these, e.g., from within the school, from the LEA or from parents and other interested members of the local community?

(xv) Is there adequate monitoring of progress and regular reassessment of special needs?

(xvi) Are parents properly informed and advised, more particularly are they fully *involved* as far as possible in meeting the needs of their own (and possibly other) exceptional children?

(xvii) In a high technology age, is full use being made of modern aids and equipment in the interests of exceptional children, or is it still legitimate to counter demands for more (and more modern) equipment by the old jibe that what has been supplied has never been effectively used?

(xviii) What more can be done in the primary schools to provide for greater 'continuity' between the pre-school/primary and primary/secondary stages?

The range of questions could, no doubt, be extended almost indefinitely. It will cost a lot of effort and resources to produce better answers than have so far been contrived, but it costs nothing to go through a check-list and identify those areas where changes are possible and likely to be beneficial.

Any discussion of exceptional children in primary schools will inevitably include very frequent reference to specialist expertise and the general class teacher's need for advice and support from specialist sources within and outside the school. But one thing seems entirely clear. The future quality of primary education will depend critically on the quality of the general class teacher, who is the pivotal point around which all else must revolve [as Leonard Marsh, Mike Hill and other contributors to this book emphasise]. He must continue to be a fully responsible, highly trained, competent professional, coping (like the general practitioner in medicine) with all the day-to-day problems as they arise. But he must also (like the general practitioner) learn to develop, and use more effectively in a wider context, his own specialist knowledge—and he must learn more about the problems and challenges of exceptional children and about when 'outside' help really *is* needed and how to get it. There is nothing in Warnock (or, for that matter, in any other recent educational reports in this country) which is designed to achieve the 'paralysis of the generalist', and it will not serve the interests of exceptional children, or anyone else, if the general primary teacher gets the idea that *every* problem requires specialist attention outside his competence. Our primary schools need more and more effective specialist support; they do *not* need a 'specialist take-over'.

References

Butcher, E. and Dawkins, J., 1979, 'Bringing secondary specialisms to primary schools', *Education,* 153 No. 5

Central Advisory Council for Education (England), 1967, *Children and their Primary Schools,* London, HMSO

Committee of Enquiry, 1978, *Special Educational Needs,* London, HMSO

Department of Education and Science, 1978, *Primary Education in England: A survey by HM Inspectors of Schools,* London, HMSO

TEACHER DEVELOPMENT

9

Teacher Development:
pre- and in-service education

Derek Sharples

Why Bother?

Turmoil has long been a way of life in teacher education. The succession of changes from the fifties onwards has included the rise and fall of the large single-purpose colleges (in England at least), the wax and wane of the teacher education bulge, the birth and death of qualification patterns (two- and three-year certificate and 3 + 1 'old' style B.Ed's), the honeymoon and divorce between the universities and many colleges. In the state of change which is here to stay the first wave of revised B.Ed. degrees is recruiting students, and many college buildings, refurbished and extended in the last ten years, are accommodating new occupants—from refugees to post office technicians, town and country planners to demolition gangs.

In an astonishingly short period of time teacher education has been transformed from a situation where it was largely conducted in single-purpose colleges with a student population of modestly qualified young people with guaranteed employment, to one where it is carried out as a minority activity in institutions characterised by much broader academic and social concerns, with a student population no less well qualified than most other undergraduates and sharing with them a problematic future. Moreover, the control of many of the institutions where teacher education takes place is no longer held by

107

erienced school teachers and teacher educators. The particular demands for resources and time in teacher education
have to compete in the increasingly fraught arenas of large,
complex institutions against the demands of widely different
concerns, from post-doctoral research in polymer science to
teletype operating.

Now all this may well be for the good. The isolation of
teaching and teacher education from the 'realities' of many
other occupations had long been criticised; tempering teacher
education in the fire of more critical and open validation
procedures and institutional demands certainly appears to
improve its resilience and lend it a sharper edge. However, the
dissolution of the old order, the disbanding of its professional
association, its loss of control of its context, give rise to a whole
range of issues for concern. Some of these are explored later in
this chapter, but it is a matter of urgency that the central issues
of primary schools are openly rehearsed amongst all concerned
so as to provide a background of informed professional debate
against which current changes and challenges in teacher education can be set. Judgments affecting the nature of the professional education of primary teachers are being made almost daily
in the validation procedures, resource decisions, staffing policies and development proposals taking place within higher
education. It is essential that these judgments are informed by
a clearer articulation of professional demands and development
in schools. Though qualitative changes in primary schools will
largely be brought about by the teachers within them, the
lively and principled provision of appropriate professional
education at all stages is also essential.

Touchstones

More years ago than I can imagine possible I was a member of
a group whose tutor demanded that we summarise *Primary
Education* (1959) in two words, and she proceeded to lay about
us when we failed to produce the two she had in mind. ('Time'

and 'quality' they turned out to be, not 'primary' and 'education' after all.) Were I to indulge in a similar exercise in relation to teacher education in the 1978 primary survey, 'competence' and 'judgment' would be the two hurrah words for me.

Explicit reference to professional development is scant, but a review of the survey's implications for the rôle of the primary teacher throws more light on the needs recognised by HM Inspectorate. Direct reference to the need for a 'pattern of in-service education and training' to support teachers follows the familiar arguments raised in the Plowden and James reports. The notion of 'pattern' is not explored, although the breadth of providing agencies is recognised and the importance of school-based in-service work is stressed. Competence and judgment are emphasised in these recommendations, which suggest the major function to be the development of competence in terms of content mastery and téaching skills, and the enhancement of judgment in terms of expectations of pupil performance and definition of the curriculum. An additional function is that of developing professional leadership amongst teachers holding posts of responsibility, with once again a stress on content mastery and professional judgment. Allied to this is the concern for such teachers to have skills of curriculum leadership, consultancy and development at school level. These recommendations have their roots in the survey findings of low levels of subject mastery amongst primary teachers and the related observations on the potential influence of teachers with special responsibilities on the one hand and their inhibited penetration in many schools on the other.

Initial teacher education, the survey suggests, should ensure competence in a core curriculum, including analytic understanding of the nature of the content and a command of such professional skills as instruction, planning and communication. Particular stress is again placed on specialist areas of expertise in content, linked to abilities to develop specialist work across a school curriculum. Judgment is emphasised in two areas, the appropriateness of expectations of pupil performance and

109

capabilities, and the selection of relevant teaching strategies and pupil activities. The recommendations arise from the survey findings of restricted teaching and learning styles in many schools, but more notably from the disparities found in 'match' between pupil capability and teacher expectation. Some of the assumptions behind the findings, not least the reliability of the 'match' procedure, are open to considerable question, but the recommendations do not depend upon particular findings alone but on assumptions concerning the rôle of the primary teacher, his competence and judgments. In the following sections this will be further explored, on the assumption that the improvement and clarification of teacher professionalism implied by the recommendations are both provocative and desirable.

Plowden recommendations in the same area present a sharp contrast. Many of the problems addressed in 1967 were quantitative; more, longer, deeper and broader were urgent concerns. More than half of these Plowden recommendations have been or are being achieved: there has been an enquiry into teacher education (whatever one's view of James, it was,) most initial teacher education is in diversified institutions, O-level maths is to be required of all teachers, an all-graduate entry is round the corner, graduate exemption from professional training has almost ceased, schools and teachers are becoming more involved in teaching education, salary scales have been revised, in-service degrees are widely available and school management courses are developing at a number of levels. Interestingly, the Plowden recommendations for regional in-service planning, and improved links between initial courses and the needs of schools remain matters of concern in 1979.

Perhaps of greater significance, however, is the contrast between the professional model implied in Plowden and that in the 1978 survey. The professional definition and status implied by the proposals for teacher aides in Plowden provoked extreme reaction and defensiveness under the banner of

110

'dilution'. Whilst the abortion of the proposal was politically complex, a significant factor was the vulnerability of the profession of primary teaching to the threat posed by intelligent and sensitive, if formally unqualified, participants. Current emphasis on competence and judgment amongst teachers, and for a recognition of professional hierarchies, where amongst a given staff each will play leadership and followship rôles in different curriculum areas, raises the issue of professional structure again, but in a more demanding form less open to simplistic resistence by a protectionist lobby. Special responsibilities in Plowden were conceived with much less sophistication than in the 1978 survey, where responsibilities are related to central professional activities of planning, assessing, diagnosing, instructing, task and target setting, and self evaluation—all demanding high levels of competence and judgment.

A further significant contrast between the two reports lies in the general assumptions of the teacher and the curriculum. The 1978 survey is to some extent a reaction against the social romanticism of the Plowden Report [as Robert Dearden suggests in Chapter 2]. References to the importance of curriculum content are more rigorously stated, attitudinal and social issues are seen alongside concerns for fundamental learning and for practical and communication skills. Evidence of the relative independence of class size from achievement and of the limitations of teacher autonomy in the survey raises doubts about some assumptions in Plowden; emphases on standards, evaluation and accountability replace emphases on organisation, social compensation and autonomous professionalism as safeguards of quality.

Teacher education has had its own reports which have coloured developments between 1967 and 1979. The James Report (1972) fulfilled the Plowden demands for an enquiry into teacher education. Its financial implications were overtaken by economic difficulties: action in relation to its recommendations was frustrated by a number of factors, both internal and external to teacher education. Despite its problematic reception at a difficult time James's stress on recurrent in-service education was farsighted and generous overall. Its insistence on academic rigour restored the importance of content mastery, though it was less sensitive to problems of professional skill acquisition and the particular needs of primary teachers. *Education—a framework for expansion* (1972), which proved to be a guideline for retrenchment as far as teacher education was concerned, was the second administrative document to affect teacher development. Subsequent trends, coupled with changing patterns of aspiration amongst school leavers, have overtaken its plans. Although since 1972 a small number of erstwhile colleges have made a promising start as diversified institutions, there remains much uncertainty for the future. Problems of resources and student numbers rather than principle and purpose are likely to dominate change and adaptation in the mid 1980s.

Silver Lining

As with falling rolls in schools (Chapters 13 and 14) the current circumstances of teacher education do provide opportunities as well as problems. Of considerable significance are the effects on the competence and judgment of training institutions. Reduced numbers of students and rigorous validation procedures conducted by the Council for National Academic Awards (CNAA), have produced fresh levels of maturity and rigour in colleges. Procedures for the systematic involvement of teachers in course planning and validation have begun to improve a traditionally difficult area of relationships. This has been greatly assisted by the requirement that two-ninths of college-based teacher education has to be in the in-service area. Teachers and tutors are now exploring common issues, with more school teachers developing insights and skills, enabling them to play active rôles in initial training on the one hand, and more college tutors developing direct concerns for school competencies on the other. As in-service

112

provision in colleges develops there is a tremendous opportunity for local and regional development of clearly articulated structures of in-service education, professionally oriented and providing inter-linked courses and development work at all levels; from school curriculum groups to masters degrees and group research projects. Regional distribution of this in-service resource should be especially valuable for the support and encouragement of school-based, and school-initiated, in-service activity.

Equally important will be the effects of falling rolls and the consequent stability in primary school staffing. The tendency for professional education to be associated with professional advancement in terms of promotion will be replaced by a concern for the enhancement of professional action, for improving the competence and judgment of teachers in their present positions. An increasing level of professionalism, signalled by the growing proportion of graduates of Open University and in-service B.Ed. courses and by the achievement of an all-graduate entry to primary teaching, should give rise to still more school-related development. A further effect of falling rolls should be the development of exploratory patterns of organisation within and between schools, which should facilitate the development of staff with special skills [as illustrated in Chapter 14].

Falling rolls in and amongst colleges are having a salutory effect on the supply of primary teachers. Those entering teacher education from 1980 will have made a particular decision for professional preparation; already the great majority of college students possess the entry requirements which qualify them to be on other degree courses. Security of occupation, with employment rates still around 65 per cent, is no longer a crude motivation; opportunities for higher education are no longer restricted. Students in teacher education will provide an able and committed pool of recruits to the primary schools. The reduction of demand for teacher education staff in initial training will enable schools to retain colleagues with

113

interests and abilities in professional education, further enhancing their potential for school-based work and particularly for the development of induction programmes located in schools and classrooms, which is where they should be.

The Melting Pot

For both pre-service and in-service education the major issue needing urgent debate is the meaning and significance of professional competence and judgment. Of prime concern must be the emergence of a professional dialogue, of increased communication between and amongst teachers and tutors, of a professional language of principle, practice and evaluation rather than an occupational forum for description, anecdote and procedure. Within such a dialogue the relative potentials and responsibilities of schools and training institutions must be developed. High on the agenda must be an expansion of the summary teacher competencies suggested in the primary survey—knowledge of children, sensitive adjustment of learning programmes, co-ordination and balancing of the curriculum. The assumptions underlying class teaching and the teacher's rôle in the development and maintenance of the school curriculum must be commonly agreed if there is to be an improved 'match' at the level of professional education in relation to practice. As another important agenda item, teacher education must help the profession face, and answer, demands for accountability and for evidence of effectiveness in terms of appropriate and relevant pupil learning. Developments in teacher education will be judged in terms of their effectiveness in promoting such learning.

Immediate action is needed to resolve the differential patterns of in-service provision and to provide a means by which teachers can directly influence, contribute to and benefit by, their development. The increasing separation of public and university provision presents an added difficulty. Despite the problems, and they are considerable, co-ordination of professional education especially at the in-service stage must be a major priority.

At an institutional level emerging issues concern the relationship of schools to the demands of individuals and society, and the relationship of teacher education institutions to the demands of schools and school teachers. Key issues need resolving or clarifying. What is primary education about? What do its teachers require in professional skills and knowledge? How are schools to be judged? Following some resolution or clarification of these issues, or alongside them, can be considered the particular issues of teacher education. At what stages in professional development are particular skills required? What are the most productive functions of teachers and tutors? How are the contributions best co-ordinated?

Excelsior!

Longfellow's young man had an enviably clear orientation; the shibboleths of competence and judgment do not have comparable directness in the landscape of teacher education. 'Onwards and upwards' is a poor substitute for cartography, and the foregoing discussion has outlined many of the hazards which figure in the terrain. However, some principles of direction can be suggested.

Of prime importance is the development and maintenance of the growing professional dialogue amongst all concerned, with a continuing responsibility being encouraged at school level. The professional committees of colleges, in-service policy groups of local authorities and management groups of teacher centres provide immediate forums for positive and co-ordinated planning, but their agendas must be illuminated by a corporate agreement on criteria and an informed awareness of professional needs. Emphasis must be placed on the development of mastery in professional skills, evaluation and subject matter. Teacher Initiated Professional Studies might sensibly begin to lend new meaning to TIPS for teachers.

115

Action research at school level, co-ordinated among schools by in-service agencies, should begin immediately to establish the particular meanings of competence and judgment in specific settings [Christopher Saville's chapter offers one possible model]. Involvement in this could provide the roots of both an appropriate local in-service structure and a practical rationale for initial education. An inevitable by-product would be the emergence of an appropriate professional language in which the varied experiences of teachers could be considered in terms of professional action rather than in the esoteric language of much educational research.

A longer term objective must be an improved policy and planning body for teacher education. Enhanced professionalism might give rise to a more coherent and positive initiative from teacher associations; implementation of some aspects of the 'Oakes' proposals for a new advisory and coordinating body at national level would provide such a forum. The demise of the universities' functions and the absence of DES proposals to replace them have left a frequently observed gap in teacher education. Currently, battle lines are being drawn between rival groups involved in higher education; in the growing struggle it will be essential to ensure that the coherent education of primary teachers is a triumph of whatever victory rather than a casualty of whatever campaign.

References

Committee of Inquiry, 1972, *Teacher Education and Training*, London, HMSO

Department of Education and Science, 1972, Cmnd. 5174, *Education: a framework for expansion*, London, HMSO

Department of Education and Science, 1978, *Primary Education in England: A survey by HM Inspectors of Schools*, London, HMSO

Ministry of Education, 1959, *Primary Education*, London, HMSO

10

Staff Development:
a research-based model

Christopher Saville

'In-Service Training is partly given through attendance at specially designed courses, but also takes place within a school through observing others at work and through discussion with fellow teachers and particularly the head, teacher trainers, teachers' centre wardens, visiting advisers and inspectors and others.' (para. 8.55 *Primary Education in England*)

The concept of school-based or school-focused in-service education is not new, although its elevation to the status of a vogue is new. As with most developments, definitions abound and the merits of siting in-service work in the school depend upon whoever is making the claim. To a greater or lesser extent most schools actively engage in developmental work, be it only at the level of staffroom discussion. The purpose of this chapter is to take a critical look at some of the existing patterns of in-service provision and to offer an alternative model based on the concepts of school-based research and a process model of accountability. I shall attempt to show that shifting the site of the provision is in itself not sufficient to meet the needs of schools and teachers.

Purposes

What is the purpose of in-service work with teachers? If the existing array of provision is examined a number of purposes can be deduced ranging, for example, from the dissemination of new

117

curriculum materials to the development of management skills. A variety of agencies are involved, from the Schools Council to the professional organisations and local education authorities. The teacher might well ask where he fits into the patterns of the providers and what rôle he has to play in the definition of his classroom needs. This chapter contends that the methods employed in determining needs and providing in-service experiences are of equal importance to the content. Whilst many of the perceived problems facing teachers and schools relate to content or knowledge, an equal number relate to skills or processes [to competence *and* judgment, to use Derek Sharple's terms]. The external providers have traditionally focused attention on 'new ways'; new curricula, new materials, new courses, new projects, new methods of organisation. Many of the recent curriculum projects have been based on classroom evidence but [as Leonard Marsh points out in Chapter 16] this evidence has been lifted from the site and processed elsewhere, thus losing a basic sensitivity. Alternatively, some developments have taken the line that a framework should be defined externally and the teacher left to develop the flesh of the material for himself. As an adviser I have often heard teachers talking about in-service experiences. The majority have told of enjoyable, interesting courses, of good fellowship and good ideas. Another usual plea has been for something practical, no high-brow theory. These common statements allied to classroom observations have led me to look closely at the type of courses which I was organising and to examine more critically the question of purpose.

Self-evaluation

Working closely with a colleague we developed over three years a policy of rigorous evaluation of our courses. This policy included the use of several experienced external evaluators, our own questionnaires and post-course observation and interviews. Several important issues emerged and we were able to begin to determine a theory of our practice. It was this process of (self-monitoring through performance) evaluation which caused us to reappraise our work. If we could begin to answer some of our process problems in designing and running courses, would the model work as well with teachers in schools? The difficulties as we appreciated them were vast; many we are still working on. For example, the problem of need definition was, and still is, dominant. To start with we found that none of our researches illustrated in measurable terms a sustained change or changes as a result of our courses. Talking to teachers six months after a course which, according to our earlier evaluation, the teachers had rated very highly, we found that whilst the course was remembered, sometimes for bizarre reasons, very few changes had resulted in terms of classroom action. The best that we found, to our dismay, were cosmetic changes to organisational practices. This implied that we were expecting and looking for changes of a more profound nature without having previously determined what those changes ought to have been as a result of the course. In turn this also suggested that we had assumed an authority of wisdom on schools, and teaching to which we were not entitled. Our courses were in themselves an assumption that we had an answer to the intricacies of every situation. This left us in a dilemma, because just as our evaluations indicated that our practice was not successful in our own terms, teachers were strongly in favour of being given 'answers' to 'practical' questions.

The process of evaluation caused us to rethink and helped us to identify several issues.

a The issues of identifying needs and purposes.
b The question of balance between instruction and enquiry.
c The problem of expectation and perception of in-service provision.
d The need to create conditions within schools and classrooms for evaluation practice to develop, thus providing teachers with evidence on which to articulate their in-service needs.

Without realising it at the time we had come full circle to a definition of our purpose and aim in in-service work. This was that our rôle as external agents must be an enabling one, that our perception of teaching and schools was born from our own experience and practice which could not simply be passed on by adopting an instructional methodology. Whilst we might have had certain skills, knowledge and values we felt it necessary to balance these with the need to develop enquiry-based methods. However, a crucial dilemma remained: the majority of teachers taught in a didactic manner (as confirmed in the DES primary survey) and there was no reason to suppose that secondary teachers were fundamentally different in this respect. We deduced that there was an expectation of what courses should be and what methodology they should employ based on teachers' own practice. We too, had been on courses where frustration and boredom prevailed or where the message to be open-minded was given without the right to question or discuss. Put another way, we felt that much of what was on offer to teachers by us and others was attempting to answer process or methodological problems with packaged, unanswerable products. The Green Paper (1977) spoke of developing 'lively enquiring minds' as one of the aims of schools and most teachers would endorse that aim as a target in their work. What that statement demanded was an exploration of curriculum methodology as much as a consideration of curriculum content. But in order to begin that evaluative questioning we came to the belief that schools and teachers needed the basic enabling condition of confidence. This confidence we defined as a recognition of existing practice which tended to be of a didactic or instructional nature.

A Model

As a consequence, our model of in-service work begins from an acceptance that the base line or starting point is didactic teaching. The model recognises teachers' expectations of in-service courses and of advisers and is divided into three phases.

The beginning of phase one is highly structured with an agenda largely determined by ourselves, although based on evidence from previous evaluations and observations. The course documentation and the style of teaching is authoritative in nature, structured in content, or as one course member reported, 'Like an ICI management course'. The presence of the external evaluator from the beginning is a signal of intent. The purpose of this design is basically twofold. Firstly, it indicates to teachers an instructional methodology par excellence; the use of visual and technological aids in addition to a packed and busy programme builds a confidence and develops motivation and identity. The second reason is equally important in that the agenda is designed to develop skills aiming particularly to enhance the teachers' ability to recognise issues and articulate them. The event is 'practical'. We use simulation exercises based on researched evidence, thus reinforcing a sense of reality in relation to school and classroom issues. This first phase usually lasts four days at the local teachers' centre, with a programme designed to begin with us providing 'answers' and raising issues from our experience and knowledge and leading to the participants bringing in their own perceptions, skills and knowledge. Put alternatively, it begins as a course and ends as a conference. The importance of the external evaluator cannot be over-stated; from their evidence we have gleaned a great deal of practical information in determining balance and timing, as well as in indicating gaps between our intent and our practice. Sooner or later the purpose of our evaluation is raised and becomes part of the agenda, leading to the whole concept of research and evaluation in relation to work in schools and classrooms. In this we have been much impressed with the work of John Elliot and the Classroom Action Research Network based at the Cambridge Institute of Education.

The second phase builds on the first and is based in schools. Each course member is given the option of undertaking a study of some aspect of his work or the work of the school. We have found great difficulty with the use of the word 'research'; many people have been put off, conditioned we suspect by the problems of language and the traditional separateness of research on education. There has been widespread anxiety that teachers could not

121

match the quantitative methodologies associated with educational research. We have attempted to overcome this by avoiding the use of the word 'research', substituting for it the word 'project' and by sharing with the group our own efforts of evaluation. There have been two further problems. Firstly, we have been concerned that teachers would undertake some school-based work which might be just in order to please, cynically termed as 'psychophantic intent'. The fact that we are concerned with appointments and preferments is a serious problem and we could do no other than to recognise the problem. (Interestingly, as the group of participating teachers have grown from course to course, this is an issue that we have been able to discuss openly.) Secondly we have been concerned in case the projects might avoid contentious problems and be rather self-deluding in nature. This has proved to be true in part. Headteachers for whom we have run management courses have tended to be much more cautious in selecting topics than classroom teachers—understandably so, though many have chosen difficult and sensitive issues. Advice and support is given during the phase of problem identification although we are cautious about being too specific methodologically. For the most part, teachers' topics have not been self-deluding, and if anything the level of crtical questioning has developed too fast, especially when the topic has concerned individual teachers looking at their own classroom work. It should be emphasised that at no time is pressure applied either implicitly or explicitly either to undertake a project or to produce a report.

The third phase takes place about three months after phase one. A one-day meeting is held at the teachers centre where course members can present and discuss their work. Sometimes this is a verbal report with no supporting evidence, although in most cases papers are produced and circulated with supporting tapes, films or questionnaires. At this meeting we share the report of the external evaluator. The discussions range from specific issues arising from the papers to a discussion of the purposes, problems and issues of school-based research work. We emphasise in phase one that the project should be selected for personal or school usefulness; it is not intended as an academic exercise. Not all the course members undertake projects, not all of them are successful, not all of them are even completed. Many teachers complain of not having time, as well as the usual problems of access and fear of upsetting other people. Most teachers recognise the value of researching their own work or aspects of their institutions whilst at the same time producing data on problems and constraints. Above all, our evaluations indicate that the process of questioning is the most powerful and sustained element.

The Thinking School

This began with the concept of school-based in-service work. I want to end it with a reference to the concept of the thinking school. If a school is to develop this concept, then it has to look at the manner in which decisions are made and how its actual practice relates to its perceived aims and process of decision-making. It is no good for people who are external to the school determining aims without addressing themselves to the means by which they can be accomplished. Too often, the manner in which schools are resourced means that those appointed to posts of responsibility are effectively unable to carry out the aim of the post itself. How, for example, can a teacher appointed to be head of language development in an infant school carry out curriculum development work without evaluative evidence? This she will find difficult to collect because she has a full-time teaching commitment. The model I have described is limited in effectiveness because collectively we have yet to recognise that research is an integral part of a teacher's rôle. A thinking school needs evidence, evidence for decision-making and evidence for accountability. Some might say that this should be the work of the adviser or the inspector, but I would deny this. It is the process or act of self-evaluation which is important as a prelude to

123

innovation and the ingredient which will sustain that innovation. The rôle of the external agent is to enable that process by developing the necessary research skills, by acting as the support and consultant to the process and by being a moderator or critical questioner. This implies a new rôle for the provider of in-service work; he can no longer be the unquestioned bringer of the latest 'goodies' either from Schools Council or some management service agency. That is if the providers genuinely believe that the purpose of in-service work is, in the final analysis, to improve the educative lot of children.

References

Department of Education and Science, 1977, *Education in Schools: a consultative document,* London HMSO

Department of Education and Science, 1978, *Primary Education in England: A survey by HM Inspectors of Schools*, London, HMSO

11

The Teacher's Craft and 'Basic Skills'

Mike Hill

'Teachers, parents and others are inevitably and rightly concerned with the standards achieved by children in school. It must, however, be recognised at the outset that there is no one standard which is appropriate to all children of a given age. Individual children vary in their capacities and abilities, and some children perform moderately in one area of the curriculum and yet show good ability in another.' (DES 1978).

As primary education moves into the 1980s it comes as a surprise to read that the Inspectorate still consider it important to restate the case for the child as an individual learner. For in that one simple statement about children is contained implications for the nature of the curriculum, initial training and continuing development of teachers. There are also implications about the organisation of the school, staff and time-table, on what is to be taught, and how it is to be taught, and to whom.

The Plowden Report refers to 'the best of primary education'. The 'best' is based upon vision and upon certain ways of thinking about children learning. It has been brought about by the vision and practice of head teachers and class teachers closely supported by sympathetic administrators, who to-gether determined to create conditions and relationships in which children could as respected individuals most effectively and happily learn. But from the vision to common practice? From the inspiration to administration? How long does it all take? The vision has existed for many years but the time has never seemed quite right for it to become legalised. The half-century since that watershed of educational thinking, the 1931 Hadow Report, has seen radical changes in society. The rapidity of change is certain to accelerate with bewildering speed as this century moves into a technologically-determined age, an age which will demand even more the qualities of adaptability, open-mindedness and flexibility. In such a society where most knowledge will have built-in obsolescence, the tradition of a school as a place where a fixed body of knowledge has to be learnt will become increasingly irrelevant. It will make even more relevant the Hadow Report's perhaps now too familiar phrases, 'the curriculum is to be thought of in terms of activity and experience rather than knowledge to be acquired and facts to be stored. Its aim should be to develop in a child the fundamental human powers and to awaken him to the fundamental interests of civilised life.' What will be considered a civilised life for the 10 year old of today at the middle peak of his life, say in 2005? Today's electronic communications systems could appear rather like a coach-and-four does to a Concorde traveller. Technology could at its present stage of development replace much of the repetitive manufacturing and office work done by the manual work force. The manufacturing work force could wither as dramatically as the agricultural work force did during the industrial revolution. Alternatives will have to be found for the existing work ethic. There will be greater leisure time for physical and intellectual pursuits to be followed and these will have to be catered for. Schools have an important part to play in preparing pupils now for full participation in this very different kind of society.

The survey suggests, 'However the requirements of society come to be formulated, teachers have the main responsibility for responding to them', and that 'the curriculum is probably wide enough to serve current educational needs. But the demands of society seem likely to continue to rise—priorities may well change within these areas [literacy and numeracy] and in other parts of the curriculum. The immediate aim should probably be to take what is done to greater depth.' (DES 1978). How can this be done and the deficiencies noted in the survey remedied? It will be to the detriment of primary education if taking 'what is done to a greater depth', is considered in the traditional light of an accumulation of facts, through the completion of exercises in textbooks. This will lead only to further superficiality, already found by the survey in those areas of the curriculum requiring understanding of what historians, geographers, scientists, craftsmen actually do as performers, problem formulators and problem solvers in their search to understand the world we live in. What is important to the growth of the primary child is not a particular fact or a particular group of ordered facts but the method or the process of acquiring them. It is the mastery of the process by the child which has to become the major concern of the teacher. Skills and ideas have to be identified by teachers, advisers, inspectors, and incorporated into the curriculum [as Joan Dean and others point out]. There is no need to insist upon any particular field of human interest or subject discipline; indeed, the wide-ranging interests of the child have to be used more frequently as the major vehicle for learning.

The survey supports the view that skills of observation and experimentation should be common to many aspects of the curriculum, and yet finds that observational or experimental work is not at all common. This hardly suggests that the curriculum is being thought of in terms of 'activity and experience' by the majority of schools. Those items of the curriculum found by the survey to be treated superficially, if at all, are those very areas that demand as a prerequisite the skills of observation. For the geographer, scientist, artist, craftsman and historian, the careful observation and recording of the observation in symbolic form is a 'basic skill'.

127

If there is to be any deepening of the existing curriculum as suggested, then observing must become such a recognised 'basic skill', equal in importance to the traditional 3Rs, but ranging wider into the broad curriculum. It will not be from the basis of a limited number of science specialists in schools that progress in primary science will come, nor from existing in-service training methods. Observational skills will provide the practising classroom teacher with the beginnings, indeed the very roots, of a scientific approach to the curriculum—a curriculum that needs to be based firmly in the reality of the child. It is the transformation of the commonplace, a building, a flint, a brick, a bicycle gear, insect or plant that will provide the starting point. If time is given to observe with care, if time is given to question, with the child held firmly in the security of the relationship with the trusted adult, then this will provide child and teacher with the springboard for progress and growth in science and in other areas. It is from seemingly commonplace things that the content of the curriculum needs to be found.

In only a small minority of the classes inspected during the survey were observational skills noted to any degree. In Plowden's 'best' it has been commonplace practice for some years. The practice in these schools where close observation and the expressive arts go hand in hand is not new, but is the result of some very basic and simple beliefs; respect for the individuality of children, respect for their work and belief in experience of reality as the basis for learning.

Are teachers with specialist knowledge in particular curriculum areas another way of meeting the deficiencies noted in the survey? It all depends on what is meant by 'specialist'. If schools are basing experimental and observational work on wider-ranging investigations of the environment, provision of specialists to cover the multiplicity of disciplines required would be impossible to achieve. However, if the potential of teachers already in the schools is identified and encouraged to develop by headteachers and advisers, many enthusiasms as yet undiscovered will provide the school with their 'specialists'. They will be specialists in the sense of being dedicated, knowledgeable enthusiasts who influence by example, who influence through discussion, who influence through trust and belief in their colleagues. They will begin with their strength, the children in their care.

The survey also suggests a degree of staff redeployment to improve work in particular areas. Is it worthwhile increasing the size of registration groups to enable a teacher to be freed to work alongside his colleagues or to take smaller groups for particular purposes such as teaching children to make coherent arguments or how to take part in discussions? It may be desirable, but this has to be balanced by the need for children to build up strong consistent relationships with one teacher. Even if schools consider it desirable, they will need much convincing that this can be done without much better teaching ratios than the tight staffing schedules operated by most LEAs.

The survey devotes some space to discussing children's performance on standardised tests. Although assessment is vital [as indicated in Chapters 3 and 5], education is *not* only about performance on NFER tests. It is about total growth, the individual growth of each unique being in our schools, both adult and child. For many of today's children, growth in school begins with the consistency of human relationship, with the acceptance of the persons that they are. The fact that they can be accepted as useful, needed members of the community, perhaps because they check the pencils daily or care for the animals without ever forgetting, enables them to gain a worthwhile self-image. With that self-knowledge of worth, teaching can be effective. The survey gives some recognition to this aspect of the teacher's work in its section on 'The General Setting for the Work', but does not go far enough to emphasise this vital intrinsic part of the primary teacher's rôle.

No matter how supportive the administrators and advisory services or how constructive and vigorous the teacher trainers, it will be the quality of professional diagnosis, treatment and personal relationships in the classroom that will determine the degree of progress in the final two decades of this century. It will be the class teachers' conviction in, and knowledge of, their rôle which will eliminate any deficiencies noted in the report and will answer public criticism [as Leonard Marsh's contribution acknowledges]. Teachers will need to be continuously reconsidering their rôle and developing their skills in the light of the *needs* of their clients, the children. The wants of parents, industry, secondary schools, politicians and of the press and television will all be pressed on primary school teachers. Of whom should they take notice? Where will they find their convictions? The source of that conviction will be found when they diagnose and treat the needs of children at nine o'clock on a Monday morning—needs that will be set by the human and physical resources of the school, through the disciplines of being and doing.

Although extremely important, understanding, warmth, sympathy and knowing what needs to be done, are as nothing if teachers are not able to do the *job* of knowing when and how to apply the wide range of practical skills necessary for competence in their craft. Success and professional competence will only result from an understanding of the possible learnings in any given experience and a much greater attention to detailed planning. A child recording the fine workings of a closely observed clock mechanism with a blunt stub of pencil will certainly learn something of how his teacher values that experience. With the survey's suggestions for teacher development including 'the importance of teaching children to observe carefully', and the acquisition of 'a sound, even if restricted range of practical skills in science as well as in art and crafts', I agree with Roy Storrs that it is more imperative than ever that teachers attempt those skills themselves, so that they might appreciate something of the nature of the experience they are offering children and be better able to plan both for the time, material and support that will be necessary. This is as vitally important for the already 'trained' teacher as for those in training. How often are children asked to write a poem, do a drawing, work with clay, paint, observe closely and record, write a story, by adults who have never experienced these disciplines? For many teachers it will mean a personal searching for a competence to enable them to do a job properly, a job for which the majority have been inadequately prepared. The occasional topping-up at a course, used to gain tips to survive the immediate future, is no way to prepare for the demands of the '80s.

As stated previously, teachers will have to share their gifts and interests and this is how they will need to be thought of as 'specialists', and headteachers will have to be helped to identify competence and good practice and put other teachers in touch with excellence where it is to be found. They in turn will need help in identifying good practice in other schools and help in organising in-school staff development, thereby helping to sustain the morale and career satisfaction of teachers whose opportunities for advancement will be more limited than ever before and whose security, due to contracting rolls, will be threatened. Despite the problems that will have to be faced in increasing the awareness of heads and teachers who have not perhaps yet considered development as a professional commitment, the opportunities and the pointers forward are clear. Teachers have an opportunity to show that they can raise their performance mainly by their own efforts by looking critically at their present practice [as Christopher Saville points out in the previous chapter]. Good teachers have always faced up to the major problem of trying to understand what it is like to be a child learning in their classrooms. Those responsible for guiding and supporting teachers will have to try and understand what it is to be a teacher in a classroom, trying to understand what it is like to be a child learning.

The finest preparation for the present and the future is an active response by teachers and children to their experiences of reality. Such a response will bring mastery in the present and go on to enthuse learning and growth for the future.

References

Consultative Committee of the Board of Education, 1931, *The Primary School*, London, HMSO

Department of Education and Science, 1978, *Primary Education in England: A survey by HM Inspectors of Schools*, London, HMSO

12

Children's Social Experience: a framework for primary education and primary teacher education

Alan Blyth

Children's experience is essentially social. From the earliest days in the family, they learn and grow in interaction with others. What is more, this interaction is itself of central interest and significance for them. It matters to them how they relate to others, for this is crucial to their self-image.

Social experience is more than a mere succession of discrete events, since a child's memory constantly re-interprets events, itself developing at the same time, so that his self-image also undergoes continuous revision and in its turn modifies the child as actor when he encounters further experiences. There is in this process a unity, somewhat akin to the unity of action postulated by dramatists or by phenomenologists[1], that constitutes a child's developing identity. This unity is complex, developing by spurts and pauses and even regressions, but its general direction is towards greater maturity and greater potential. For each individual child, meanwhile, the process is unique.

This social experience is a framework within which primary education is developed. It begins before primary education, it surrounds primary education, and secondary education, and it continues long after both. By selecting this continuity of social experience as the principal framework for primary education, it is possible to see primary schools in fuller perspective. Within this framework, they are neither total institutions, absorbing the entire life-space of their pupils, nor are they terminal institutions, bringing children merrily to the age of eleven or twelve or even thirteen, and then disclaiming responsibility for what happens next. But they are essential institutions, since if life does not end at twelve, it certainly does not begin at twelve. Investment in secondary or tertiary education cannot compensate for deficiencies in primary education. Nor is it sufficient to regard primary education as elementary education, on top of which secondary education can be piled, as though it were a separate package containing rather more valuable goods. If education is to be successful, there must be prolonged and systematic interaction between individual children's social experience and a curriculum designed to engage at all stages with that experience, as fully as possible.

To adopt such a standpoint is not, of course, novel. It belongs in some measure to many educational traditions; to all, in fact, that have been concerned with education in a full sense. In the Christian tradition, social experience continues from life into eternity and primary education constitutes a brief, but decisive, intervention in that process. To Rousseau and his successors, the art of primary education has been that of adjustment to the growing individual organism; to the Herbartians, a necessary means of shaping its development. But it was from Dewey and his followers that children's *social* experience first received due emphasis, in two important ways: as a determinant of education, and also as a component of education. During the twentieth century, the first of these two emphases has come to be widely accepted and it is now a commonplace of progressive education, especially in the primary years. The Plowden Report epitomises this first emphasis.[2] But it does not fully or coherently endorse the notion that children's social experience is a component of primary education as well as a determinant. It does not bring out the elements of intervention and interaction implicit in a fully-developed social-experience framework for primary education. This is a further step, requiring some analysis of the continuity of social experience itself as it develops and is modified within primary schools.

When children first go to school, they enter two new worlds, the classroom and the playground.* The first is the embodiment of formal education; the second is a significant modification of the very social experience with which formal education interacts. In learning to be pupils, children have to adjust to both worlds; and the world of the playground may well be the sterner of the two. Moreover, parents are well aware of this. By using terms such as 'rough kids' and 'stuck-up snobs' they indicate reluctance to commit their own children to several years of social experience without considering the company that they will keep. It is scarcely surprising to find that, in the Plowden survey, proximity to home was cited as the most prominent reason for parents' choice of primary school, followed by denominational status, good local reputation, and family connections.[3] Clearly, when choosing, parents may have had a short, safe daily journey in mind; but social experience must have counted too.

Once they are launched within nursery or infant schools, children develop relationships within both of their new worlds. The pattern of these relationships depends partly on external influences, partly on internal features within the schools. The interaction between the two is complex.** To take one familiar scene as an example: Jane shouts something rude at Jean in the playground. Maybe this piece of verbal

* To be sure, some schools would claim to have no classrooms and no playgrounds, only open-plan spaces and green fields. But the terms still stand as symbols for the formal and informal contexts within a school.
** Many studies have been made of the interaction between internal and external factors. A representative selection can be found in Woods, P. and Hammersley, M., (Eds), 1977, *School Experience*, London, Croom Helm. It is noticeable that most of the chapters in this volume, and most of the authors from whom it draws, concentrate on relations between children and teachers rather than on social experience among the children themselves.

aggression is the result of family tensions; maybe it reflects behaviour approved in Jane's sub-culture; maybe it is an indirect protest against the teacher or the school, or just because she suddenly does not like the look of Jean's face. Nobody quite knows, not even Jane. And nobody knows how Jean will react. Social experience is never entirely predictable.

Yet Jean has to learn, for herself, how to respond to Jane in a manner that will build up her own self-image. To ignore the other child is a non-response; to cry (even if she only just manages not to) is babyish, as she already knows. So she gradually develops a repertoire of responses which have currency within her social group. She has already begun this process of social learning in the family and the neighbourhood, but the entry into the new social world of school may well involve a peremptory intensification in that process, impelled by imperatives besides which the carefully-contrived class-room invitations to language and number are mild and gentle in comparison. This social learning has no Fletcher textbooks, no Schools Council projects, to assist it. Instead, it depends on a curiously self-contradictory process. For the very children who exact their savage penalties from those who fail to learn also offer example, and often encouragement, to those who try. They are all in the same existential predicament, busy growing up, and learning clues from siblings and slightly older peers which earn them temporary prestige. This process is largely concealed from adults; it has to be, since one of its goals is to attain independence from adults, though parents and teachers are partially aware of it and occasionally an assiduous researcher, suitably camouflaged, and equipped with anthropological insight, penetrates a little farther.[4]

There are limits to the guidance which children can give each other. It can be made available only within the limits of their own culture. If Jean is severely handicapped, or highly gifted, or coloured, or has unusual interests, or belongs to a very different social group with different customs and mores and accent, then the rest of the class may lack the resources to cope with her needs and she faces the danger of exclusion, a fate which the architects of neat schemes for social mixing are prone to belittle.

For most children, the process develops adequately. As sociometric studies reveal,* school classes become welded into societies with distinctive patterns of behaviour whose practice, interacting with the school curriculum and organisation[5] imparts a sense of collective identity. This is expressed in shared jokes and rituals, all the more effective if they appear absurd to outsiders, and also in experiments in resistance toward adults. Then, girls and boys begin to draw apart and to establish their sex-identities, regrettable though some people now seem to find that process. Meanwhile, usually first among girls, small tightly-knit groups begin to emerge, while the class as a whole develops leaders and dominant individuals (not necessarily the same people) and leaves others, whether from their own choice or perforce, to remain on the periphery. To some extent this in-school process, which extends into early adolescence, reflects what is going on in neighbourhoods[6] but primary schools remain, to some extent, autonomous theatres of social action.

Within the matrix provided by this sequence of social experience, primary schools introduce the planned intervention that is known as the intended and hidden curriculum. This curriculum is an authorised version of reality and its outcome depends on its interaction with the children's social experience. Any group of children develops, from its social experience, a distinctive attitude to the curriculum, or perhaps several differing and even conflicting attitudes. Teachers soon discover what those attitudes are. Children who fail to respond to their teacher's signals may do so not because they have

---

* Although sociometric studies can only reveal a partial picture of children's social groups, they are invaluable for this limited purpose and still regularly used. The generalisations embodied in an early study are still largely valid. See Blyth, W. A. L., 1960, 'The sociometric study of children's groups in English schools', *British Journal of Educational Studies*, 8, (2), 127–47.

misunderstood those signals, but rather because they have understood only too well the signals from the other children.[7] This can even affect the learning of basic skills, but it is more marked in other parts of the curriculum.

For example, schools claim to influence attitudes[8] and the evidence from *Primary Education in England* indicates that they do.[9] Statutory R.E. is itself intended to achieve this among other aims. Yet it is evident that schools can only affect attitudes insofar as the curriculum interacts with the social experience that the children already have. This process cannot be accelerated beyond a certain pace. Even if some individuals can attain a moral precocity that would astonish Kohlberg, they are just as likely to be mocked and dismissed by their peers as insufferable prigs.

Much the same is true of positive knowledge and understanding of the physical and social environment, especially the latter. It is true that mathematics, science, art and the social subjects all arise largely as patterns and differences are indicated and perceived in the environment, but the alacrity with which children respond to these curricula developments depends in its turn on the importance which their previous social experience assigns to them. To some extent, as sociologists have insistently reminded us, this is a matter of social class: the subject curriculum belongs to middle-class culture and is more readily accepted by middle-class children even when they poke fun at it. What sociologists have emphasised less is the way in which these social-class differences are mediated through groups of children. For this social process brings out the cross-voting patterns that are present. It identifies which middle-class children do the poking fun, and which working-class children find a new and more universalistic world through the curriculum, and how they in turn influence their peers.

The selection of a social-experience framework for the consideration of primary education implies a further perspective on the curriculum. For it indicates that one element in this planned intervention in social experience concerns the modification of that experience itself. Children become aware of themselves as growing older and stronger, socially more sophisticated, and intellectually more capable. The art of the curricular 'match' is to present challenges, not only in physical education but throughout the curriculum, which are just beyond the children's present reach so that they discover the satisfaction, fun, and joy of accessible achievement [as Wynne Harlen points out in Chapter 5]. This, too, must be related to previous social experience and the evidence from *Primary Education in England* suggests that the estimate of what children are capable of doing is often, for one reason or another, ungenerous.[9] One such reason may well be the extent of demands made on individual teachers' capacities. Another may be the difficulty of striking a practicable balance between three considerations: the need to respond to community beliefs that schools, especially primary schools, should be what Willard Waller called 'repositories of ideals';* the need to avoid keeping children unnecessarily young; and the need to adjust to children's social experience. The physical layout of a primary school, and its social organisation, often express just that difficulty. Built and organised as a little paradise, it is peopled with children who sometimes feel whirled along too rapidly and sometimes talked down to. Different children experience these reactions differently. Secondary schools meet the same problem literally writ much larger. Middle schools, where they exist, can help to ease the transition from the one to the other.[10]

This brief discussion of primary education in a framework of social experience emphasises the extent to which the adoption of such a framework implies also a choice of values. There is a

* Waller, W., 1932, *The Sociology of Teaching*, New York, John Wiley, ch. 4. This institutional expectation is not vitiated by changing expectations of teachers' behaviour as suggested by Boothroyd and Cohen: Boothroyd, K. and Cohen, L., 1972, 'Willard Waller revisited: some reflections on parents' expectations of teachers', *Journal of Curriculum Studies*, 4, (2), 154–7.

very real sense in which the framework is the message. By emphasising the continuity as well as the validity of children's social experience, this framework suggests not only that formal educational institutions do have limitations, but also that they ought to have limitations. The curriculum can, and should, interact with social experience rather than dictating it. Such a view goes more readily with a liberal-democratic theory of education than with others. Today, it is open to challenge.

On the one hand there is a growing demand for a more functional approach, one which looks for measurable outcomes. Conscious of the explosive expansion of knowledge and of its uses, and also of the national need for increased productivity, the advocates of this viewpoint would substitute for the framework of social experience a framework of accountability. Proper accountability is of course necessary within any framework, but that is a very different matter from viewing accountability itself as a framework. For this could imply a narrowly functional interpretation of primary education and a concentration on secondary and higher education. That would be self-defeating in two ways. For one thing, as was indicated at the outset, the later stages in education are dependent on enrichment at the early stage. Secondly, it would be self-defeating in another sense because it might involve concentrating on measurable skills like subtraction, which can be hived off to calculators, rather than on social understanding, which cannot, and which depends on judgment rather than certainty, without which mathematical competence may be wrongly directed. In a social-experience framework, social understanding could never be omitted; but in an accountability framework, it might.

The other challenge to the social-experience framework is a framework based on ideology. It is graphically epitomised by a little boy with an angelic face and a loaded rifle. From a social-experience standpoint he is the victim of a hideous perversion of childhood; but to the committed freedom fighter he is the heroic vindication of a principle, who, unlike the

140

incorrigibly bourgeois Lost Boys in *Peter Pan*, is using a real weapon alongside real men and women. Even if few advocate such an ideological framework for primary education in England, there are many lands where it is encouraged or even imposed by force, and it would be rash to claim that it could never happen in Belfast, or still nearer home.

In contrast to the accountability and the ideology frameworks, social experience offers something which is richer in quality, more realistic, and more humane. The others are cheaper and simpler. They are also less demanding on teachers, for they posit straightforward tasks while the social-experience framework requires each teacher to be both a social scientist, able to analyse children's experience, and an artist, able to devise a curriculum that can interact with that experience, enrich it, and improve it. This is the 'new professionalism' of which so much is heard nowadays in the field of curriculum development and innovation. It depends on those qualities which were traditionally associated with the 'born teacher'. Sir John Adams, in a familiar phrase, once emphasised that the verb 'to teach' governs a double accusative: I teach John Latin.[11] We all know that the curriculum, the official reality of today, is in its totality much more demanding than Sir John's Latin. We also have to remember that, in a social-experience framework, the teacher of today has also to understand more completely not just Sir John's John, but also Mary, and his friends, and hers, and how they interact with one another. In fact the modern teacher has to govern not just two accusatives, but two whole clusters of accusatives. To achieve this depends partly on ability; partly on pre-service and in-service training, to which *Primary Education in England* pays welcome attention[9] [as does Derek Sharples in Chapter 9]. But the second capacity, the understanding of children, arises essentially from the continuity of teachers' own social experience, stretching back to their own childhood and interacting with all the formal education they have received. Such experience is likely to predispose teachers to want to study children in

141

order to educate them better. It is noticeable that teachers nowadays are generally much more favourably disposed than they once were to consider, in a spirit of constructive criticism, the outcome of the upsurge in research into the development and education of younger children which has characterised the past twenty years. The Plowden survey, the Schools Council research and development programme, major research programmes in institutions of higher education, and many instances of exploration and research by teachers themselves, are symptomatic of the coming of age of primary education as an academic study which, alongside the outcome of practical experience, can enable primary teachers to hold their heads high as members of a profession with a respected basis in scholarship. And it would be justifiable to claim that the outcome of this scholarship tends to vindicate, and to be vindicated by, the social-experience framework.

In the last analysis, however, the choice of framework depends on the choice of values. The social-experience framework seems to me to provide a more comprehensive view of primary education than its rivals. It also seems to me to be associated with preferable values. It sets individual children in the midst, but it does not leave them there. Grounded in reality, it denies omnipotence to primary education, but it encourages that enrichment of its activities which *Primary Education in England* appears to vindicate.[9]

References

[1] Curtis, B. and May, W. (Eds) 1978, *Phenomenology and Education*, London, Methuen, especially the Introduction

[2] Central Advisory Council for Education (England), 1967, *Children and their Primary Schools*, London, HMSO, Vol. 1

[3] —Vol. II, Appendix 3, esp. p. 127

[4] Morgan, J., O'Neill, C. and Harré, R., 1979, *Nicknames: their origins and social consequences*, London, Routledge and Kegan Paul

4 Opie, I. and P., 1959, *The Lore and Language of Schoolchildren*, London, Oxford University Press

4 Roberts, A., 1978, 'Extraversion and outdoor play in middle childhood', *Educational Research*, 21 (1), 37–42

4 Sluckin, A., 1979, 'Avoiding violence in the playground', *Educational Research*, 21 (2), 83–8

4 — *Growing up in the Playground*, London, Routledge and Kegan Paul

5 Hallinan, Maureen T. and Tuma, Nancy B., 1978, 'Classroom effects on change in children's friendships', *Sociology of Education*, 51, (October), 270–82

6 Blyth, W. A. L., 1965, *English Primary Education*, London, Routledge and Kegan Paul, Vol. 1, chs 3, 4

7 Root, Jane, 1977, 'The importance of peer groups', *Educational Research*, 20 (1), 22–5

8 Ashton, P. *et al*, 1975, *Aims into Practice in Primary Education*, London, University of London Press

9 Department of Education and Science, 1978, *Primary Education in England: A Survey by HM Inspectors of Schools*, London, HMSO

10 Blyth, W. A. L. and Derricott, R., 1977, *The Social Significance of Middle Schools*, London, Batsford

11 Adams, Sir John, 1907, *The Herbartian Psychology Applied to Education*, London, Batsford

IN THE EIGHTIES

13

Falling Rolls

Howard Collings

The number of pupils in maintained primary and secondary schools in England and Wales has grown from five million in 1946 to reach a peak of nine million in 1977. As a result of the continuous fall in the annual number of births between 1964 and 1977, the overall school population started to decline in 1978. This decline will continue for at least a decade, the fall in school population being at least 1½ million over the period. By the nature of the educational system the effects of changes in the size of age groups of children are seen first in primary schools and then some five to six years later in secondary schools.

Four factors are involved in determining the projection of the number of pupils in schools:

a the projections of future births and the resulting population projections by age;

b the projected number of pupils of compulsory school age;

c the projected number of pupils under five;

d the projected number of pupils over compulsory school age.

Three main sources of information are available to assist in revisions to projections of school population. First there are projections of the numbers of live births and population by age for future years prepared by the Government Actuary's Department. Secondly, the Department of Education and Science carries out a census of the numbers and ages of pupils in schools in January. Thirdly, there is a DES survey of the previous year's school leavers.

147

Projections of the population of England and Wales by sex and age have been made by the Government Actuary's Department since the 1920s. The Actuary makes a single principal projection each year on the set of assumptions that seem most appropriate considering the statistical evidence available at the time. The value of a single 'official' projection is that it provides a consistent base for the many users of the projections. However, in forward planning it is often valuable to examine the consequences of making different assumptions about the components of the projections. In educational planning, assumptions about differing death rates are of minimal interest. Migration assumptions are important at local authority level but have a very small effect at the national level. However, varying the fertility assumptions can have a dramatic effect upon the size of the future national school population. In recent years the Government Actuary's Department, in conjunction with the Office of Population Censuses and Surveys, have published variant population projections which offer some measure of the effect of uncertainty about fertility rates used in the principal projections.

No matter how much detailed data are available to assist in population projections or the refinement of the techniques used, a projection is based on assumptions which are almost certain to be inaccurate to a greater or lesser degree, even though at the time of making the projection they may have been judged to be the best that could have been made. Bearing in mind the large changes that have occurred in yearly numbers of births over the last two decades, it is instructive, before considering the latest projections, to examine how well those school population projections which are determined almost entirely on births made over the last twenty years matched up with actuality.

Fig. 3 shows the projections of the 5–14 year old age group in maintained primary and secondary schools in England and Wales made in 1955, 1961, 1965, 1970 and 1975. As would be expected, all the projections are fairly accurate up to seven years ahead, since births will be known for all but two of the age cohorts. However, beyond seven years ahead the projections soon lose accuracy and by fifteen years ahead show a very wide divergence.

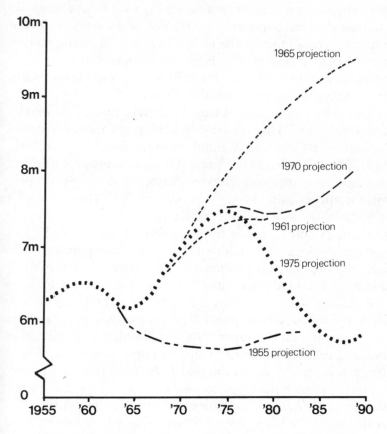

Fig.3 Pupils aged 5 to 14 in maintained Primary and Secondary Schools (England and Wales), and projections (DES 1979)

In 1955, there was a history of a 'trough' in the annual number of births following a rapid decline from the 'post-war bulge'. The 5–14 school population was expected to decline slightly and then level off throughout the 1970s and 1980s. By

149

1961, however, it seemed clear from the rapid upturn in births which had occurred, that following a small decline in the early 1960s there would be a sharp climb in pupil numbers and then a levelling off in the 1970s. In 1965, with births at a very high rate, the prospect was of continuing high births and a rapidly increasing school population for the rest of the century. It is of interest to recall that in the early 1960s official demographers were being criticised for being too conservative in their projections of future births. By 1970, with a continuous decline in numbers of births over the previous five years, it was projected that a turn-round would then take place, followed by a gradual rise. The resultant school population projection indicated a stabilisation in numbers in the late 1970s and early 1980s (the fall in births not being sufficient to produce a decline in school population). With the further and steeper drop in birth numbers since 1970, there was by 1975 a prospect of a substantial fall in the school population by the late 1980s of the order of $1\frac{1}{2}$ million pupils from the then current total. Projections made since 1975 indicate a 5–14 year old population in the late 1980s below that predicted in 1955 (just below 6 million) and over 3 million fewer than the projection made in 1965.

In recent years the Department of Education and Science have published school population projections in their series 'DES Reports on Education'. Report Number 96 published in November 1979 is the latest giving pupil projections. Fig. 4 (from this report) shows the mid-1978 based principal projection and two variant projections of births provided by the Government Actuary's Department. Also shown on the chart is the mid-1974 based principal projection which incorporated an assumption that in the long-term the average number of live births per woman would be 2.2. The mid-1978 based principal projection followed the mid-1975 based and intervening year ones in reducing this long-term assumption to 2.1 (which in the long run would lead to the population just replacing itself). The two variants shown were based on different assumptions about fertility:

(i) a high variant assuming a rapid reversal of the decline in births after 1978/9 to reach replacement level in 1981 and an average of 2.3 live births by the middle 1980s.

(ii) a low variant assuming a further decrease in annual births to 1980 followed by a comparatively slow turn round to an

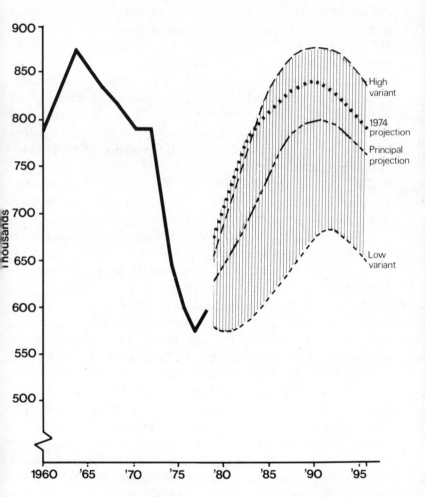

Fig.4 Births in each year—England and Wales 1960 to 1978 and projections to 1996 (DES 1979)

average of 1.8 births (the annual fertility rate of two years ago) in the second half of the 1980s.

Actual births in 1978 were above the projected figure of the mid-1977 based projection and higher than the total recorded in 1977 but below that of the mid-1974 based projection. Births registered in the early part of 1979 confirm that the low point in the annual number of births might have been reached in 1977 and indicate that the high variant projection line may turn out to be close to actuality for the next year. However, it would be premature to assume that the continuing high variant projection is more likely to reflect the pattern of annual births in the 1980s than the other projections. The rapid and sustained increase in fertility rates implied by the high variant projection requires more confirmation than the evidence of birth numbers for eighteen months.

DES Report on Education No 96 discussed three separate elements which go to make up the projection of the total number of pupils in maintained nursery, primary and secondary schools in England and Wales. The number of pupils under compulsory school age was projected to rise from around 350 thousand (in full-time equivalent terms) to just below 500 thousand over the next fifteen years.

The Report made projections of pupils over compulsory school age based upon the proportion of pupils who would stay on after reaching the age of 16 and referred to the alternative projections of this element made in Report on Education No 92. The variation in projected numbers resulting from the assumptions used for pupils both below and above the ages of compulsory schooling have an insignificant effect upon the projections of total school population as in any year around 90 per cent of pupils are within the ages of compulsory schooling. However, the separate projection of these relatively small elements of the total are important because of their implications for the provision of buildings, teachers and other resources.

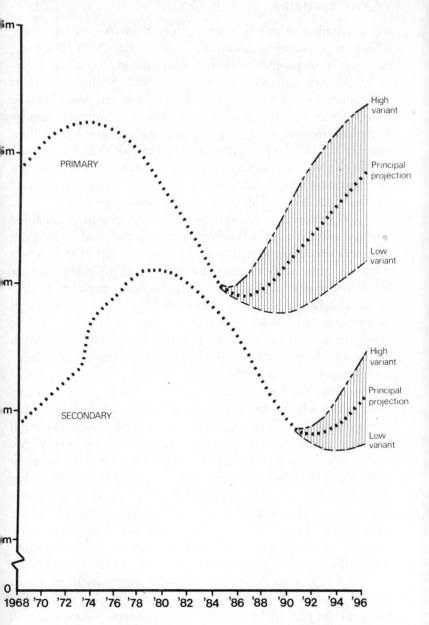

Fig.5 Primary and Secondary School population (DES 1979)

153

The number of pupils in maintained primary and secondary schools is projected to fall until at least the late 1980s (assuming the high birth projection holds). Considered separately, however, the primary and secondary trends exhibit important differences over time. As Fig. 5 indicates, the shape of the wave pattern of fall and subsequent rise in numbers is similar in each sector but whereas primary numbers have been falling since 1973 secondary numbers reached a peak in 1979. Because pupils numbers are so closely linked to births there is bound to ·be a comparable difference in the timing of an upturn in pupil numbers between the primary and secondary sectors.

In 1973 there were about $5\frac{1}{4}$ million pupils in maintained nursery and primary schools in England and Wales; by 1979 numbers had fallen by half a million. As a result of the known numbers born each year up to the end of 1978 one can be virtually certain that a further fall of 1 million pupils will occur in these schools by 1986. After 1986 primary school pupil projections are more uncertain as they become dependent upon children as yet unborn. If future births follow the high projection there could be by 1996 as many children in nursery and primary schools as there were in 1973.

However, the recent upturn in births has been an expected event although the prediction of the year in which it would occur has been difficult. There has always been an expectation by demographers that fertility rates would eventually rise again. The fall in fertility rate since 1964 has been attributed in part to couples postponing the start of family formation rather than their decision not to have children at all. Even if fertility rates remained constant a rise in annual births would be expected as throughout the 1980s there will be an increasing number of women of child-bearing age in the population. Thus, although the rise in births in 1978 and the latest figures for 1979 appear to be in line with the high variant of births shown in Fig. 4, future birth numbers might well move towards the principal projection line and even below it during the 1980s. If this occurred pupil numbers in nursery and primary schools in 1996 might rise to around 4½ million; about half the increase which would occur if the high birth variant held.

Over the last twenty-five years the number of primary schools has remained fairly constant (around 23,000) and the average number of pupils on the school roll has fluctuated much in line with total pupil numbers. There has been a significant reduction in the percentage of schools with less than 50 pupils; from 22 per cent in 1950 to 8 per cent. The proportion of junior-with-infant schools has also fallen over the last twenty-five years with the fall becoming more marked since 1973.

It might be considered surprising that the total number of primary schools has not fallen since 1973 in view of the fall in pupil numbers. Were it not for the unprecedented fall in numbers and the speed of the fall yet to come, an argument could be advanced for the number of primary schools in 1986 to be the same as now. However, the average school roll would then be about 155 compared with 224 in 1973 and 210 now. Less than 5 per cent of primary schools would then be likely to have more than 300 pupils compared to over 20 per cent now. The proportion of schools with less than 50 pupils would almost certainly rise. The average size of an individual age group in a school would drop from 40 now (it was around 45 in 1973) to just below 30, implying that a significantly increased proportion of schools would have less than 20 children in an age group, which could lead to a large increase in the number of children being taught in mixed-age classes [as discussed by Norman Thomas on page 16].

Of course, it would not be possible to reduce the number of schools in proportion to the reduction in pupil numbers. In some cases falls in pupil numbers will mean that temporary accommodation need no longer be used and in others it could mean the end of over-crowding. Even if some 10 per cent of existing schools were to be closed by 1986, it would be unlikely to increase the proportion of schools with more than

300 pupils. The most likely effect would be to lower the proportion of schools with less than 50 pupils and raise the proportion with between 200 and 300 pupils. The average school roll would be raised to around 170 and the average size of an age group per school would be 32, but with a lower proportion of small schools the incidence of mixed age teaching would be significantly reduced from what it would probably be if there were still 23,000 primary schools in 1986. There are bound to be significant increases in those unit costs of primary schools which are attributable to aspects other than the teaching staff employed. Where pupil numbers are falling there will be unavoidable diseconomies in the cost of running a school. These arise largely because the costs of the premises—the wages of caretakers and cleaners, outgoings on repairs, and on heat, light and water, tend to be generated by the existence of the school accommodation itself rather than by the number of pupils using it. There is also expenditure on other non-teaching staff such as administrative and clerical staff which is not proportionately affected by changes in pupil numbers. It has been estimated that only about one quarter of the expenditure (excluding teacher salaries) in running a primary school can be related to the number of pupils, three-quarters arise because of the existence of the buildings.

A further problem to be considered in looking beyond the fall to the possible rise in primary pupil numbers, arises from school closures. If numbers are likely to rise again questions arise whether it would make sense to keep schools open for ten or more years with greatly reduced capacities (and at increased operating costs) or should schools be closed and kept in mothballs. Obviously, individual decisions taking account of all circumstances will have to be made for each school, but the indications from studies of population movement do suggest that many areas of population growth occur in 'greenfield' sites requiring the provision of new services. The risk of mothballing schools is that when pupil numbers rise, the extra pupils will not be living near these schools.

156

Just as a contracting education system has diseconomies of scale in its use of non-teaching resources it will also have diseconomies in its use of teachers. It is not practicable for local authorities to reduce the number of primary teachers at the same rate as the fall in primary pupil numbers. Even when pupil numbers in a school have fallen to the extent that there are more teachers on that school's staff than its entitlement would have been on previous criteria, there will be many circumstances where the redeployment of a teacher may take time or, sometimes, be impracticable. In some cases, for example where a head teacher retires, a replacement would be necessary even if the school already had more teachers than entitlement.

In addition to the above problems resulting from school rolls becoming smaller, extra teachers are needed as a result of schools being smaller. As previous paragraphs have illustrated, even if some schools were closed the average size of primary school would fall markedly. In practice smaller schools now have, and will need in the future, more generous pupil–teacher ratios than larger schools of the same type and age range to provide the same standard of education. This is partly because a headteacher's administration time forms a greater proportion of total teacher time in small primary schools.

This chapter has sketched out the fall in the primary school population as far as it can be reliably foreseen and indicated the wide range of estimates that are possible when future births have to be used to project primary school numbers. It is not possible here to do more than indicate the consequential effects upon the number of schools that will be needed to house these pupils and the number of primary teachers who will be employed. It can be seen from Fig. 5 that the fall in primary pupil numbers will be much steeper in the early 1980s than experienced so far. It is likely, therefore, that if teaching costs are not to rise substantially, the scale of teacher redeployment will need to be greater than hitherto. In the early 1980s, secondary pupil numbers will be falling also and thus opportunities for redeployment to the secondary sector seem less likely. However, if primary numbers

157

do rise appreciably in the late 1980s, this will be at the time when secondary teacher redeployment is likely to be at its maximum.

Reference

Department of Education and Science, November 1979, *Trends in School Population*, Report on Education No. 96, HMSO

14

Working in Smaller Schools

Roy Storrs

Much attention has been focused recently upon small rural schools because of the intended closure of many of them. Various action groups, supported by the National Association for the Support of Small Schools, have made extensive use of the media to extol the virtues of small schools in an attempt to effect their reprieve. It is perhaps regrettable that the problem has been forced into the public arena, as small school closures are not peculiar to the 1970s. Under the 1944 Education Act LEA's were required to provide a development plan for primary education and since then, in my own authority, there have been sixty primary school closures, twenty-five of these since 1965. The decision to sustain these closures was made by the DES after long and detailed discussion and was devoid of undue acrimony. The wisdom in taking this course of action, often to create more viable amalgamations, cannot be denied.

The small-school debate has been given prominence and will be prolonged by the declining birthrate, which will severely effect the rolls of primary schools [see Chapter 13]. It has been predicted that, by the mid 1980s, there will be 32 per cent fewer children in our primary schools than in 1974, and even the 20,000 extra children born in 1978 will only reduce this prediction to 31 per cent. As a result, the problem of steep decline will extend to urban as well as rural areas. That this situation is already with us to some degree was highlighted by Mrs Williams, former Secretary of State, when at the North of England Education Conference in 1979, she said

159

'The first consequences of that decline [in population] are visible in the half-empty classrooms in the infant schools of some of our new towns and big local authority estates as well as in inner city areas.'

Most schools, then, will be smaller and this could have a detrimental impact upon the primary curriculum unless urgent steps are taken to plan positively, but realistically, for the future.

It is gratifying to note that *Primary Education in England: A survey by HM Inspectors of Schools* (HMSO 1978) places great emphasis upon the curriculum. During the last decade attention has been so much upon organisation and method that consideration of the attitudes, skills and knowledge which primary children should be developing has become secondary rather than fundamental. The survey has, therefore, adjusted the focus whilst at the same time recognised the need to relate what children learn to how they might be supported in their learning, by its less prominent reference to approaches and organisation.

The survey is critical of the range and implementation of work in primary schools, recommending a broad curriculum in which children should be given the opportunity to use and develop competence in the basic skills through application in other curriculum areas. This demands a considerable shift in attitude for many teachers, who, because of the difficulty of being masters, or even jacks-of-all-trades, or because of their own limited vision, severely restricted children's experiences. That teachers are also found to be less capable of providing an appropriate level of work for children of average and above average ability adds a further source of concern in relation to the smaller schools. HMI attribute this mis-match, in part, to mixed-age groupings (which will soon be difficult to avoid in most schools) and to the lack of specialists in the various curricular areas (which will be equally difficult to provide).

How to improve the curriculum offered to primary pupils

nvolves a careful assessment of both the opportunities and the problems presented by falling rolls. Except at the very extreme, the problem is not one of actual school size but of the way falling rolls affect establishing ways of organising schools and working with teachers and children.

Opportunities to be Grasped

Too often the opportunities presented by smaller schools (of whatever actual size) are overlooked, but certainly there are advantages to be gained [as indicated by Tom Marjoram in Chapter 3]. As the numbers of children fall, schools will be able to maintain many of their existing resources of books, equipment, apparatus, and, above all, space, but for fewer children. The survey finds that the range of work in some classes is inhibited by adverse physical conditions, the most prevalent being the lack of space. The vital question concerns the use of newly available space, which is likely to be in the form of a spare classroom. Such a room could be used as a general-purpose room facilitating a range of activities such as music making, withdrawal group work, and, if blacked out, drama, viewing TV or films (which in many schools would free the over-worked hall). It could be used as a place where parents can meet in discussion or undertake ancillary work in support of teachers. It could act as a store for resources, as a room for rearing small animals, or if suitably furnished, as a room offering facilities for activities requiring more specialised equipment and materials such as science, mathematics, cookery, art, craft or even photographic processing. An example of such a room is described in *Art in Junior Education* (1978).

'Someone had the vision to give it [a spare classroom] new life by making it into a craft workshop and store. It is more than this—it is a kind of working museum as well. There are old glazed drain pipes, pottery chimneys and an Edwardian sewing machine embellished with gold transfer decoration.

161

These objects, and many other natural and man-made one
are arranged on open shelves to encourage handling an
close examination. This is a place for activity, a room we.
organised for making things, not somewhere just for stand
ing and staring. Areas are clearly defined, for clay, for wood
for metal and for print making.'

As a second illustration of an initiative taken on the question
of space, I can think of a Shropshire village school built to
accommodate one hundred children, as a replacement for three
smaller isolated schools. It had three class bases, each with a
practical bay, and each opening onto a square hall space vi:
folding wooden screens. When the roll fell to fifty-five child
ren with head + 1.5 teachers there was an obvious temptation
to retreat into two of the bases. The head resisted this
however, and by having all the folding doors pushed back, he
created a large working space subdivided into areas for writing, listening, reading, mathematics, science, drawing and
painting, craft and music-making. With this re-arrangemen
and modified ways of working with pupils the whole building
became alive and the children gained confidence and a high
degree of responsibility through the trust placed in them by
their teachers.

Falling rolls also offer the opportunity to improve staffing
standards so that schools can have more manageable numbers
of children per class (thus making it easier to operate a truly
meaningful curriculum for every child) and can maintain
groups of teachers offering a range of strengths. On this
specific question it may be worth noting that, over the past
seven or eight years, the pupil/teacher ratio has improved
considerably and yet there are now fewer teachers than before
without a class responsibility. In other words, heads have
simply used the improvement to reduce actual class-sizes.
HMI suggest, however, that a re-appraisal of staff deployment
could enable some teachers to be freed of a class commitment,
thereby making it possible for two teachers to work with one

162

class at certain times. There are benefits to be had from such an arrangement, but only if it is preceded by very careful consideration as to the function of floating teachers. I have visited too many schools where floating teachers have been used simply as ancillaries, thus wasting a valuable resource.

Key Issues needing Resolution

In seeking to capitalise upon the benefits offered by reduced rolls, it would be foolish to ignore problems which may emerge.

If, as has been predicted, heads may, over an eight-year period, make only one new appointment who may then remain at Scale 1 for ten years or more, it would seem that the greatest problem to be overcome will be that of stagnation brought about by limited mobility. Understandably in these conditions a teacher's imagination and involvement could diminish, so it will be incumbent upon those in authority to help such teachers to find satisfaction within these narrow limits [as Mike Hill points out in Chapter 11].

Falling rolls will present particular problems for urban schools at present staffed with teachers, many of whom have only had experience of single-age groups. During the 1980s such schools will lose teachers and with them their particular expertise, but will gain no new blood, so may be left with older, kindly but uninspired teachers, many of whom will be for the first time faced with mixed-age groups and contact with children over a two- or three-year period. These factors may have a dampening effect upon the quality and vitality of the curriculum. Indeed, many such teachers may narrowly concentrate upon very basic skills, possibly backed by their own particular hobby horse—a 'diet' which could lose some of its attractions over two or three years. Thus a most *elementary* education may be provided, rather than the richness that is now associated with good primary practice. With the primary survey recommending a broader curriculum and inferring that

163

we must change the attitude of 80 per cent of teachers (only 20 per cent at present use an appropriate combination of didactic and exploratory methods) then teacher education needs to be a priority. This must demand professional self-evaluation [as Wynne Harlen points out in Chapter 5] so that decisions about the appropriateness of the curriculum are made as a result of clearer understanding of learning, set alongside pedagogical practice. But we know so little about what causes teachers to see the need for change, embrace new ideas, and implement curriculum development. One of my head teacher colleagues is more optimistic, seeing the increased incidence of wider age-groupings as a blessing in disguise—'perhaps, instead of moving children from one class to another because of age, this will make teachers make more professional decisions about transfer based upon the needs of the children.'

In rural schools, although often idyllic in their surroundings and in their family atmosphere, there will also be problems, but different ones. If we accept that an important part of a child's development lies in the interaction with people outside his immediate family, then the small rural school is simply lacking in numbers. It limits children's social and competitive opportunities (for example, the one single boy within the junior age range at one rural school) and can give them a false image of their own abilities (like the child who having been 'top' throughout her primary days was sadly disillusioned to find herself merely average at her secondary school). The rural school also limits the numbers of teachers to whom the children are exposed. This can pressurise teachers, who may lack professional stimulus and may have difficulty in covering a wide range of activities. Two extracts illustrate this problem:

'The ever-present difficulty of the small school is the fact that teachers have to spread their efforts so widely. . . . Much more needs to be done to strengthen and bring variety into the staffing of the small rural school' (CAC 1967).

'What is most disappointing is the failure of so many rural

schools to exploit the opportunities for initiating science which abound in their immediate environment' (Welsh Office 1978).

It is also a sobering fact that an inadequate teacher in such a school may represent 50 per cent of the staff!

The needs then are to widen the children's world, to alleviate the teachers' isolation, to increase, in some cases, the level of expectation and to support certain curriculum areas. Yet (on the one hand) these small schools already take a disproportionate amount of the available resources, and on the other, are insufficiently resourced compared to the larger urban schools. There are clearly many problems to be re-solved.

Possible Strategies

'The difficulty many of the schools have found in formulat-ing aims for some parts of the curriculum underlines the magnitude of the task facing the class teachers . . . to provide the whole range of educational experiences for classes containing children of varying ages, abilities and back-grounds. . . On the part of the teacher it requires sensitiv-ity, physical energy and intellectual and organisational abili-ties. On the part of the authority it requires the provision of adaptable buildings, a variety of resource material and equip-ment, and above all the support and stimulus which specialist expertise can provide for those who, with the best will in the world, can meet the requirements of a wide and demanding curriculum only within their own terms.' (Welsh Office 1978).

Contracting rolls only serve to highlight the need for careful resource provision and management, as undoubtedly finance will be the key factor in determining the extent of support. Authorities are already reviewing their policies and some have

165

made the decision to keep all schools open, the wisdom of which I would question. Other LEA's have adopted a policy of periodic review of small schools, accepting that there can be no fixed criteria either in terms of numbers or other factors, so that recommendations to close a school will continue to be made in the light of all known circumstances.

Whatever the policy, LEA's must consider various strategies which could be employed to maintain and improve the quality of education in their primary schools, either within their existing resources or by some additional funding. Let us again consider urban and rural schools separately, whilst recognising that there will be a degree of overlap.

The difficulties which will be faced by class teachers in small urban schools have already been identified, added to which could be the very real problem of the head, who, having been a non-teaching head for some years, may again be faced with a class commitment if the roll fell to a certain level. At an administrative level, the survey suggests that 'there does not seem to be overall, any significant educational advantage in changing during the course of reorganisation, from separate infant and separate junior schools to combined primary schools' (DES 1978). The only alternatives to that, however, would be the maintenance of existing but considerably smaller establishments, or the combination of two infant schools as a unit, and two junior schools as a unit, which would create problems of catchment. It is possible that LEA's will opt for combined J and I schools in such circumstances, recognising the benefits of the single larger unit and the economic advantage this would create across the authority. The important decisions here would be to determine the stage at which two schools should amalgamate and the fates of the displaced head and deputy.

An alternative strategy might be to maintain the smaller urban schools, thereby recognising the value of the newly available space to the school and to the community. The teachers in groups of such smaller schools might be given

166

support in the form of shared specialist teachers who could make use of the spare space, or who could work alongside the class teacher to achieve an exciting and valid curriculum. As a means of sharing expertise and maintaining enthusiasm a more positive system of redeployment (an inevitable accompaniment to contraction) encouraging teachers to move to other schools in the group, could also be considered. In adopting a group approach thought would also have to be given to the question of early admission and the possibility of competition between schools as a result of heads trying to maintain reasonable numbers.

LEA's with extensive rural areas have a problem in that they are already discriminating in favour of the rural schools. For instance, in my own authority it is twice as expensive to educate a child in a 30 pupil school and three times as expensive in a 20 pupil school, than in the average urban school. So decisions here would be different and could take a variety of forms, such as

a   an amalgamation or a replacement area school resulting in some school closures, perhaps on the retirement of some head teachers;
b   a consortium, with one head responsible for three or four outlying schools and with a larger centrally positioned building for the older children;
c   a federation by mutual arrangement.

An example of this last possibility is found in my authority where four enterprising head teachers within a geographical area of twenty square miles have found ways of co-operating for economic and educational gain, whilst retaining the advantages of their individual small school status. They have adopted the name 'Group Four' and their combined force of 200 children have shared activities in sport, music, drama, country dancing and work in the environment, with the four schools sharing transport costs. A memorable feature has been the carol service held in one of the parish churches and involving

167

not only teachers and children, but parents and seven members of the clergy—300 people in all. The four head teachers meet regularly and the combined staff meet at least once every term for educational debate, which has developed so that the infant teachers now discuss their work and make visits together, as do the teachers of the older age groups. Expensive pieces of equipment have been purchased, helped in part by the LEA, so that the children are provided with the same opportunities as are available in larger schools.

Whatever strategy is adopted, such rural schools will require further support, perhaps by area advisers who could stimulate local discussion or by advisory teachers working with clusters of schools or by extra teachers shared between groups of schools; or by shared access to expensive pieces of equipment (in my opinion the least important form of support).

Regardless of the geographical location of the schools, the most important decisions of all must be related to teacher education. Teachers must be able to state their aims clearly and to implement them successfully so that children's learning takes place in an enriched and meaningful way, in contrast to narrowly conceived, utilitarian programmes, which fail to provide opportunities for children to acquire and develop knowledge, skills and values over a broad field. As most teachers have themselves experienced a narrow, formal education, much of future in-service work should be of a practical nature so that teachers can learn through personal experience the value of the many practical activities appropriate in the education of young children. [Mike Hill's policy for staff development reiterates the same point in Chapter 11.] Assistance in this task should be drawn from local teachers or from colleges which [as Derek Sharples' chapter points out] are being directed to aim two-ninths of their teaching time to in-service provision.

The prospect of smaller schools presents numerous problems, but also the opportunity for review, leading to policies based upon fresh and imaginative thinking rather than bureaucratic convenience. Maintaining this positive stance, there is much evidence of teachers facing problematic situations, coming to terms with them and then turning things to their advantage. If we can emulate such determination and initiative by facing the difficulties of providing a broad and worthwhile curriculum in the smaller school, the future is full of promise.

References

Central Advisory Council for Education (Wales), 1967, *Primary Education in Wales,* London, HMSO

Department of Education and Science, 1978, *Art in Junior Education*, London, HMSO

Department of Education and Science, 1978, *Primary Education in England: A survey by HM Inspectors of Schools*, London, HMSO

Welsh Office, 1978, *Primary Education in Rural Wales*, Education Survey No. 6, London, HMSO

169

15

Primary Education: a radical alternative

David Oliver

The Present Situation

Parents are compelled by law to provide both the occupants and the financial support for our schools. They are entitled, therefore, to expect not only that schools do a necessary job but that they do it well. Sadly the survey, *Primary Education in England* (1978) suggests that in the initial stages at least many schools are failing in their task. As the survey makes clear, this is not because teachers lack the dedication or sense of purpose required. It is rather because the popular, inadequate model of what schooling in the initial years is about is one which most teachers share with the general public.

For years the authors of Black Papers have been demanding a return to basics, as the three R's are grandiloquently termed. What emerges from this survey and other samples of teacher opinion (Ashton 1973) is that the three R's continue to provide the core curriculum which takes up the bulk of teaching time in the majority of our schools; that 'teachers work hard to ensure that children master the basic techniques of reading and writing' and that 'mathematics is given a high degree of priority on the curriculum'. Unfortunately, teachers' perspective is just as limited to a narrow range of skills as that of their critics. So that in reading, very few children learn to read for implication as well as to locate explicit information or to follow an argument critically, and only rarely do any have the chance to develop an argument in writing. Mathematics is synonymous with arithmetic and virtually limited to computation skills, too often rote-learned. Other areas of the curriculum, aesthetics, geography, history and science are inadequately taught, and opportunities to develop a fuller appreciation of the power and application of even those skills that are taught are too frequently unrecognised or unsought after.

Reading the survey, it is not so much that one looks to Plowden for a relevant model of primary practice as to the recommendations of the Hadow Committee, made in 1931. Certainly the failure of a profession, now entirely made up of trained and certificated teachers, to improve significantly on the work of previous generations without professional training cannot do much either to strengthen the case for continued high investment in initial training, or to support the argument that school is such a necessary and valuable experience that a parent's refusal to entrust the education of his children to specialist professionals should bring him into confrontation with the legal profession as well as the educational. There are still very few schools which can honestly claim to be a 'community of old and young engaged in learning by co-operative experiment' (Consultative Committee, 1931). Yet in a time of increasingly rapid technological and sociological change there is an urgent need for this to be, not an ideal to which schools aspire, but the norm that most achieve.

The years of primary schooling are the years when a child forms a clear sense of his identity as a person in society and of his capabilities both in relation to others and in relation to the tasks presented to him. In coping with these tasks and from the feedback he receives the child develops a model of socially valued knowledge and of what it is to know which is likely to remain with him for the rest of his life and will form the context within which he develops strategies for coping with all subsequent schooling and extra-mural knowledge-seeking.

The popularly accepted view of knowledge is a content

171

view. Knowing is equated with remembering the facts selected by someone else as significant and already organised into coherent theoretical structures. The degree to which most people feel that they can have confidence in their knowledge depends not on its internal consistency or correspondence with their experience, but on how far their restatement of the corpus corresponds with some authority figure's restatement. In this way all subjects, including the sciences, are reduced to an essentially literary form. This is both an inadequate and seriously inhibiting view of knowledge and furthermore its harmful effects are exacerbated by a strong commitment to an over-complicated and in some important ways inaccurate and restricting model of child development (Donaldson 1978). Traditionally, the non-specialist primary school teachers have prided themselves on teaching children, not subjects. Plowden officially sanctioned the view that for primary teachers 'Knowledge of the manner in which children develop is of prime importance'. Unfortunately, not only is there no generally accepted model of child development but teachers have willy nilly to teach children *something* and to do this they must have access to and some adequate understanding of that 'something' they intend to present to the child's experience [see Robert Dearden's contribution in Chapter 2]. The survey highlights the fact—readily accepted by many if not most primary teachers (Wicksteed and Hill 1978)—that they lack the necessary range of subject knowledge to teach the whole curriculum on offer without a lot of specialist back-up in the form of broadcasts, textbooks or advisers. Much more disquietingly, the survey finds that these 'teachers of children' do not have an accurate knowledge of their pupils' capabilities and so too often present many of them with undemanding work. The lack of subject knowledge not so much in terms of content but of the structure of the different forms is, I would argue, the root cause for this failure to present pupils in the whole range of abilities with work at the appropriate levels of difficulty.

172

Two Responses

There are two possible responses to this situation other than simply deschooling. One involves changes in the professional structure of teaching, the other is changes in our view of what constitutes knowledge. If we insist on retaining our current model of knowledge then we need to create a cadre of senior teachers with particular areas of expertise to act both as advisers to other less well-informed colleagues and at times as specialist teachers to classes other than their own. Given both the disappointing results of the existing professional structure and training and the large number of schools too small to merit sufficient posts of responsibility there is a need for a much more radical development of this idea. It is possible to conceive of a two-tier professional structure where the bulk of classroom teaching would be done by teacher aides who had an adequate range of O- and A-level subjects and had been given a short, say three months, course of initial training in child development and classroom management. These aides would be responsible for implementing a curriculum devised, to meet truly local constraints and opportunities, by a team of teacher advisers. Each team of advisers would be responsible for planning curricula for a given population of children and for teaching it with the assistance of the teacher aides. In this system small schools could be amalgamated without losing their identity and the children in them receive the same width of curriculum as pupils in large urban schools. Recruitment to advisory teams would be from those teacher aides who had successfully completed at least three years in the classroom and would be on the basis both of their teaching and their contribution to curriculum development discussions. These people would then undergo a further three years' training on their existing salary before being promoted to adviser. Advisers' training would be academic in bias and concentrate on a narrow range of related forms of knowledge, but there would be some detailed theoretical discussion of models of psychological and mental development. All advisers could well be of equal status and paid at, say, the rates of present Grade 3. This scheme would have several advantages: it would save money, make possible a fairer and more effective distribution of resources, democratise the profession and eliminate the superstructure both of non-teaching teachers and local authority advisers, obviate the need to close small schools and enable a more flexible response to fluctuations in the pupil population.

The members of each advisory team would need to have a large say in the appointment of new members, being able at least to veto the appointment of incompatible applicants. The task of these advisers would be to plan and develop, in the classrooms where they would be used, teaching schemes and materials, to initiate the teaching of any new or modified schemes of work and to supervise and direct subsequent methods and pace of instruction. Each team would need to consist of at least four advisers, one each for maths and science, social studies, reading and language skills, physical education and aesthetics. They would be responsible for about 700 pupils in twenty classrooms across the full primary age range. The existing infrastructure of ancillary staff would not need to be altered except that the people employed in these jobs would have more authority delegated to them. No teacher would have to face the impossibly demanding task of being a full-time teaching head with advisory responsibility for all aspects of teaching in his school, or face the prospect of becoming nothing more than a too highly-paid junior clerk. Savings would come from a substantially reduced salaries bill, especially in rural areas. For those whose perspective is firmly confined to the classroom the job will retain its appeal, while those whose interests are educational rather than purely pedagogic will have increased opportunities to develop their expertise and be able to make a practical impact on the education of a larger population of pupils. I am under no illusion that this scheme will be welcomed by the powers that be, whether in administration or in the classroom. But some scheme of this kind would seem to offer the only real possibility of developing a system of advisory teachers who are actually able to advise, by giving them both the time to do so and the authority in terms of knowledge, expertise and status to push through necessary changes.

While the professional restructuring outlined above would enhance the contribution that our primary schools make to the growth of mind in our pupils, the essential reform is an equally drastic revision of our model of knowledge from a content view to a process and skills model. The need to rethink our attitude towards the nature of knowledge is absolutely essential if we are ever to be confident of devising curricula which can provide both the basis for lifelong learning and which can meet the needs of our pupils at all the stages of intellectual growth. The central concern of any teacher should be to devise materials which provide their pupils with the opportunity to make knowledge, and so develop an awareness, a gut feeling, for the tentative nature of every knowledge statement and the implicit provisos which need to be made before acting on such a statement.

Curriculum planning must primarily be derived from an adequate philosophy of knowledge and only secondarily from a manageable model of mental growth. Such a philosophy would at a general level ensure that teachers recognised the distinction between true belief and knowledge, between practical and propositional knowledge, whether the latter be *a priori* or empirical, based on reason or introspection and observation, and whether the items of information were basic or inferred. This level of insight would require teachers to know the appropriate methods of validation or falsification for each type of knowledge and to recognise in which category the various school subjects belonged. Various attempts have been made to either dispense with the concept of different forms of knowledge (the integrationist view) or to define a limited number of distinct categories (Hirst and Peters 1970). Although there has been considerable philosophical debate about

175

forms of knowledge, there is a commonsense recognition that different forms do exist, that some disciplines such as mathematics require validation by internal consistency (i.e. by reference to a coherence view of truth), while others such as the physical sciences require testing against experience (i.e. by reference to a correspondence view of truth).

The widely accepted view is that a person can claim to know 'that x' if he believes that x, if he knows the statement that x is open to validation or falsification procedures and that if following these procedures the results support the assertion 'that x'. It is also held to be necessary 'that x' be true. There is, however, no way of proving beyond doubt the truth of 'that x' when 'that x' is an empirical proposition. So what is really involved in a knowledge claim is the undertaking by the author that his statements have been subjected to and, as yet, have withstood critical scrutiny. On this analysis it is the purpose of schools to initiate pupils into an understanding of procedures for collecting data and for identifying relevant data on the basis of which to assess the strength of different sorts of knowledge claims. The pupils must in some significant way learn to be scientists, historians, geographers and mathematicians and not just memorise the results of scholars working in these fields. It is not being argued that all knowledge should be gained by acquaintance or that knowledge by description is of lower value in a school curriculum, only that teachers need the necessary conceptual background and skill to ensure that substantial amounts of time are found and profitably used to give pupils the opportunity to engage in knowledge-making skills at the appropriate level of difficulty. Such a level of sophistication will do much to prevent teachers regarding skills and content unfamiliar to them as material which must necessarily be too difficult for their pupils to learn, a mistake which lies at the root of much current mismatching of course content to pupil capabilities. Difficulty is either intrinsic to the material to be learned or extrinsic. Intrinsic difficulty is a function of the range of data to be filtered and structured, the spatial range across which and the temporal range through which an investigation is to be pursued. Extrinsic difficulty, on the other hand, is a function of the learner's physiology, purpose and experience and describes not an attribute of the material to be learned but the relationship between pupil and task. Even intrinsically easy material may prove difficult for able pupils if it is not accessible to them, that is if it is not expressed using the symbols they are familiar with nor related to structured experiences they have previously assimilated. If from the start children learn to solve problems within the confines of clearly distinguished methodologies they will gain that cognitive clarity which is an important feature in mastering any discipline.

Structuring experience or 'observing' is a function of the symbol systems the observer has available to him. From this it follows that we need to give sufficient opportunities to pupils to present their own knowledge and receive the knowledge of others in a wide range of forms which include not only language but also maps, pictures, diagrams, graphs, networks, flow charts and matrices.

What will teaching material produced on the basis of this philosophy look like? Firstly it will not necessarily use real world examples but be happy to take 'model' situations as a proper content of teaching, where data can be presented for the pupils in a manageable form. It may well be that in the early years in particular pupils will work largely from fictional material, but as time goes by new ways into even the most intractable factual material are likely to be discovered and exploited. One such fictional study I developed involved primary children reading through the description of a legendary voyage and deciding on the basis of external evidence where the events were located and how far they could be explained in terms of a distorted record of a real event. The pupils were then asked to say what further steps they would like to take to further substantiate the possible genuineness of the legend, and when the idea of parallel folk tales and the possibilities of archaeological investigation were proposed they were presented with such data to evaluate in terms of its consistency with the legend as they first encountered it and to incorporate into a more objective history of the voyage.

Such a skill centred approach does not deny or ignore the possibility of a phenomenological stance, as the following scheme, developed from reading a poem, 'The Marrog' by R. C. Scriven, illustrates. Children were first asked to draw a marrog, and write about it before hearing the poem. After the poem children were asked to draw a new marrog. The pictures were displayed and discussed. The original animal marrogs tended to be profile and the new anthropomorphic marrogs were usually shown full face; from this the idea of a schema was explored. Because certain pictorial conventions could be identified within the class, such as drawing the front and back view on separate sides of the sheet of paper, we were able to discuss the origin of new ideas and the possibility of diffusion identifying both physical and psychological factors which made adoption or rejection likely responses. Pupils were next asked to complete a matrix on which all known attributes of a marrog were listed across the top and a line provided for each person's marrog. When the different matrices were compared, no two matrices were in fact identical, although there was substantial agreement between them all, giving us an opportunity to discuss the idea that we each perceive the world differently but not so differently that we cannot recognise our world and our neighbour's world as the same. We recognised that each marrog was drawn differently and that in some, features were omitted, whereas in others extra features were included, and went on to see how far it was possible to reconstruct the original marrog by combining those features which were most recorded. An extension of this idea was to get another, younger, class of pupils to draw copies of four similar animals and to see if the older class could identify how many original models there were and how far it was possible to reconstruct their appearance. At the end of this topic pupils

178

had learned to codify data in the form of words, pictures, matrices and networks; had been confronted with the possibility not simply of error but of honest differences of perception and had been provided with the opportunity to handle conflicting data and reconstruct an 'original' stimulus–event in the manner of a historian. It is my contention that the time spent on this topic—not less than two hours a day every day for four weeks—was time well spent and gave the pupils involved a knowledge of history. It is true that the children did not learn a single historical fact but they were thinking like historians, they were learning how to learn and they were developing enriched self-awareness as to their own capabilities and the capabilities of their peers. To facilitate learning of this kind teachers do not need to cover a content-laden syllabus, but they do need to understand the deep structure of the methodologies of the disciplines.

From the description of the 'marrog' topic a second implication of this philosophy becomes apparent: prolonged discussion is extremely important. The pupils had by their own contributions to discussion significantly shaped the learning experience they had had. The pattern of learning was: identify a problem, suggest a solution, test it and state the revised problem, i.e. the knowledge-generating sequence suggested by Popper (1972). Discussion is central to any truly educational learning programme in both the cognitive and affective areas. Good art teaching requires time not only to make art objects but to evaluate them and compare judgments in a protracted and superficially leisurely way. Just as it is not enough in cognitive disciplines simply to memorise, it is not enough in the affective areas simply to make something. Critical evaluation is essential to worthwhile learning.

In this chapter I have outlined two responses to the primary survey, neither of them small-scale. I believe that the situation in our schools is such that merely to make a 'fairly modest readjustment of teachers' rôles' or minor alterations in the content and methodology of teaching is wasted effort; what is

179

required is a much more thoroughgoing revision of the structure of the profession and its accepted value system. The alternatives I have sketched seem to be required if we are to have a real opportunity within the limits of existing resources to improve the quality of the education which pupils in our primary schools receive. The one is a structural reform which can only be facilitated by the power of central government; the other is a personal but radical readjustment by teachers of their basic philosophy. Materials are readily available to provide the necessary intellectual support for such a regeneration. What is required is that individual teachers realise that it is not mere facts they need to teach, but rather that teaching children requires those in charge of instruction to understand what is really involved in knowing and how knowledge claims can be justified.

References

Ashton, P., 1973, 'What are primary teachers' aims?', *Education 3–13*, 1:2, 91–97

Central Advisory Council for Education (England), 1967, *Children and their Primary Schools,* London, HMSO

Consultative Committee of the Board of Education, 1931, *The Primary School,* London, HMSO

Department of Education and Science, 1978, *Primary Education in England: A survey by HM Inspectors of Schools,* London, HMSO

Donaldson, M., 1978, *Children's Minds,* London, Fontana

Hirst, P. and Peters, R., 1970, *The Logic of Education,* London, Routledge and Kegan Paul

Popper, K., 1972, *Objective Knowledge,* Oxford University Press

Wicksteed, D. and Hill, M., 1978, 'Is this you?', *Education 3–13*, 7:1, 32–36

16

A Forward Look

Leonard Marsh

Educational administrators will have four main preoccupations in the 1980s. First, falling school rolls will mean the possibility of school closures on a considerable scale. Secondly, questions of teacher redundancy and redeployment will arise as the educational systems adjust to the smaller number of pupils. Thirdly, the increased level of national intervention by government, together with serious financial pressures on local authorities, will raise doubts about the continuance of a locally administered educational system. Located within the debate about the effectiveness of a locally administered system (with, in the writer's view, its productive local variations in character when contrasted with state-controlled systems) there are questions to do with teacher effectiveness and the ways quality and opportunities for innovation might best be sustained in a period of national recession. The fourth preoccupation of administrators, with the national debate about 'standards', will become less and less important as the first three factors become more and more urgent in the task of maintaining day-to-day activity within the schools.

It is against this background that those with a personal interest in and responsibility for the quality of primary education will have to operate in the 1980s. The times will hardly seem promising or 'normal', but there will still be a large number of children moving through the stages of primary education and for them its importance remains unquestioned. They will have but one childhood and they deserve to be

181

taught by teachers who are skilled and confident enough to be imaginative and creative in their teaching.

Achievements in primary education have not been the consequence of expansion of resources or organisational changes. Our major investment in the last decade in curriculum projects has had little or no consequence. Such work has been developed in a different world from that of the classroom [as Christopher Saville points out in Chapter 10]. If economic restrictions are now to put at risk nationally funded curriculum projects or such organisations as the Schools Council there would be little loss from the point of view of the development of effective teaching at the primary stage. However, major problems do face those involved in primary education; a careful study of priorities and of how best to support the professionalism and confidence of the teachers is urgent if we are to make the best use of the opportunities available to us.

In his book *Children as Artists* (1944), R. R. Tomlinson wrote 'a generation ago such a title would have been considered facetious by the public and the majority of the profession. Owing to the courage and tenacity of pioneer teachers all but a few accept the title without question today.' Writing in the ill-titled publication *Art in Junior Education* (1978) HMIs state 'general progress in school depends so much on the teacher's observation of each child as the basis for planning his stages of learning'. We have inherited much. We have in England a recognition that the primary stage of education is to be seen in human developmental terms. At its best our locally administered system of education has provided the right kind of context for headteachers and class teachers to realise that recognition in tangible form. We do after all have many effective and dedicated teachers and distinguished primary schools. The over-riding question we now face is how we might best use this achievement to sustain and extend present effective practice. And we need to do this at a time of increasing parental and community interest in primary education with a sharpened demand for new forms of participation.

No longer will the headteacher be allowed to leave unsolved the problem of the less well motivated or ineffective teacher or the unwished for variations in quality of professionalism and work from one class to another within his school. The head will need to be able to answer the question 'What kind of school is it?' Parents, quite understandably, will expect 'a chance' for their child irrespective of the luck of the draw in the classes on offer. The head and his colleagues will have to accept the responsibility for developing an overall quality with a discernible pattern through the day, week and year. If teachers are to be supported in this challenging task then the local authorities will have to make more effective use of their own inspectors and in-service programmes. The LEA inspector will need a work pattern that enables him to be more than a ball boy on the centre court—always the one picking up the ball when it is out of play and never included in the game. He will need time to relate to the overall pattern of learning within the school rather than conform to an office routine that turns him into an agent for subject pressures and the like (science this year, reading without books the next).

Teaching is a process qualitatively different to that implied in much of the literature of education and curriculum studies. We need to understand the perceptions and ways of working teachers rather than regret that they have failed to devour the packaged food provided by the curriculum projects. Nor should it be a matter of concern that primary teachers have failed to use 'the theory' but rather we need to examine the failure of many to understand the significance of the day-to-day occurrences in the classroom. Our task is to support and develop the teachers' own theorising power in relation to their own work. Teachers are now required to explain their ways of working to a wider audience than ever before. They face an urgent task in developing a simple and jargon-free language that will gain support for their work and sharpen their own conceptualisation of the process. There are indications that the morale and confidence of many of the most gifted teachers is

183

now at risk. The way forward depends upon confident and sensitive teachers and we need to make more public our recognition of their crucial contribution, as well as setting about devising proper means of providing appropriate professional support.

Achievement in primary education has always been the result of practical activity on the part of a committed minority. The writer's observations lead to the conclusion that such achievement is in part the result of such committed individuals having reference to a larger cluster of people who share their vision and can bring practical illustrations to the discussions. There have been, of course, a number of minorities who have pressed upon others particular schemes such as cuisenaire rods or SRA language laboratories or the i.t.a. This kind of commitment to a device, a kit or a curriculum package such as 'Fletcher', comes and goes in some of our classrooms. In time the items find their way to the back of the store cupboard as the devotees lose interest and become disappointed with the results. But there is an essential difference between this kind of minority and the minority referred to by R. R. Tomlinson and others over the decades of primary education since the publication of the Hadow Report of 1931. This minority which has, over the years, contributed to the ideas and practical achievement of primary education has had a vision about human talents and the way people learn. It has seen in the activity of the teacher the opportunity not to teach reading but to develop readers, the opportunity to develop writers and scientists who could handle the essence, the truth of the intellectual enterprise. It is this practical achievement realised in a minority of schools which enables us to put to one side the mindless debates about specialist teachers as contrasted with class teachers and to concentrate upon a re-definition of what we mean by 'the basics'. The intellectual partnership for this activity is very much within the province of a teacher who knows a group of children well over an extended period of time (one or two years).

The primary survey indicates that three-fifths of classes have too little opportunity to use books from choice or for pleasure and that techniques in mathematics are rarely used in everyday situations. The survey also notes that children rarely drew from careful and detailed observation of things around them. We have the teacher skills and experience available to focus more sharply upon the quality of the intellectual exchange between teacher and children, child and child [as Mike Hill's chapter illustrates]. From such a close focus comes the criterion needed to produce a new definition of 'the basics', thereby ridding the primary school of its overburdened content-orientated curriculum.

This gives us our most obvious opportunity for growth in the 1980s. Its achievement will come from teachers who are encouraged to gain their satisfactions as class teachers rather than to concentrate their energies upon organisational and political issues concerned with the provision of resources. Teachers need the satisfactions that come from being in contact with the everyday development of the children they teach. Given that we can achieve this sharpened intellectual focus on the small-scale experience of children and teachers we can imaginatively respond to other tasks. There is the major task involved in seeing the school as a family centre within our communities and our society [an ideal which if realised would ease the problems raised in Joan Sallis's chapter] and the need to be sensitive to the desire of families to participate in the education of their young. We need to be aware of the social and political need to devise new ways of supporting the family in the 1980s. The 1980s could still become an era of major growth in primary education. It could well happen.

If it is to do so, teachers will have to take constructive initiatives to work out more mutually satisfying relationships with elected councillors. HMIs will need to accept that they occupy a particularly crucial place in this newly developing partnership, for there will be a need for them to state more firmly their independence within the system. They are appointed as Her Majesty's Inspectors rather than agents of their branch or a particular departmental minister. We rely upon the disinterestedness and independence of Her Majesty's Factory Inspectors in order that crucial matters of safety are not endangered by short-term commercial considerations. Children deserve their childhood. Schools at their best need to have a long-term and powerful view about people. If children's childhood is to be secured, they need to be taught by teachers confident enough to act upon their own professional recognition of its nature. This is 'the standard' that the system needs to achieve and that the Inspectorate needs to foster. As a body HMIs need to be able to give authoratitive judgments if teachers are to be freed of an undue and unproductive burden of national performance testing. HMIs need to gain the confidence of politicians in the judgments they make rather than becoming part of a pressure for testing. HMI interventions should help us all to concentrate upon the crucial factor of leadership provided by the LEA and the headteacher. The interventions should lead to a greater aware-ness of the part played by class teachers and how all of this is dependent upon some form of a locally administered service.

In the 1980s we will not be able to rely upon politicians at national level to bring a vision and breadth of understanding to education. We live in times of doubt and anxiety and politicians will be caught up with the immediate and short-term. They will have no time. If teachers through their associations duplicate the activities of politicians *they* will have no time. Instead we need to devise ways in which teachers can come together to discuss their tasks. It should be part of the task of HMIs to help ensure that nationally there is the space and scope for this to happen. And teachers in their discussions need to see that the next generation of achievements will depend upon their recognising the nature of family-centred education. It will be this new emphasis that will see teacher and elected representative working together to fashion a new relationship between elected and appointed. If teachers are professional they will reveal their commitment to the notion that children can be helped to 'strengthen and enlarge their intuitive grasp' upon the biography of their own learning.

R. R. Tomlinson in 1944 paid tribute to the courage and

tenacity of pioneer teachers. Those qualities will be much needed in the 1980s.

References

Department of Education and Science, 1978, *Art in Junior Education*, London, HMSO

Tomlinson, R., 1944, *Children as Artists*, Harmondsworth, Penguin

Index

189